Start Your Ovens

*Cooking the Way
It Ought'a Be
from the
Junior League
of Bristol*

The cookbook is a collection of favorite recipes,
which are not necessarily original recipes.

Start Your Ovens
Cooking the Way It Ought'a Be from the Junior League of Bristol

The Junior League of Bristol, TN/VA
P.O. Box 1599
Bristol, VA 24203-1599

LC Control Number: 2001-132220
ISBN: 0-9710219-0-2

Edited, Designed, and Manufactured by
Favorite Recipes® Press

FRP™

P.O. Box 305142
Nashville, Tennessee 37230
800-358-0560

Book Design: David Malone
Art Director: Steve Newman
Project Manager: Ginger Dawson

Manufactured in the United States of America
First Printing: 2001
10,000 copies
Second Printing: 2005
9,500 copies

Special Thanks

The Junior League of Bristol
would like to thank the following:

Bristol Motor Speedway—
for the cover photo and
much encouragement and support.

Special thanks to
Jeff Byrd, Wayne Estes, Sheila Long,
Ben Trout, David Rowe, and Charles Ison.

Fresh Air Photography and
Outside the Box for the cover design

Terra T. Kistner—Food Stylist

Price Photography
for the chapter photos

Special Thanks

FASTEST HALF-MILE

O. Bruton Smith

On behalf of the Junior League of Bristol, we would like to express a genuine and sincere "thank you" to O. Bruton Smith, Chairman of Speedway Motorsports, Inc., and founder of Speedway Children's Charities, for his assistance and cooperation in making the second printing of *Start Your Ovens* a reality.

Thanks to Mr. Smith, not only will thousands more get the opportunity to enjoy the delicious recipes that follow within these pages, but endless numbers of children will profit from the second printing as a portion of the proceeds generated by the sale of the book will benefit Speedway Children's Charities. Mr. Smith founded Speedway Children's Charities in 1984. The nonprofit organization, which now has chapters at each of the six Speedway Motorsports facilities, has distributed more than $12 million to agencies that aid in meeting the emotional, medical, or educational needs of children. Smith received the prestigious NASCAR Award of Excellence in 1997 in recognition of his efforts on behalf of Speedway Children's Charities.

O. Bruton Smith grew up on a modest farm near Oakboro, North Carolina, and parlayed his love for "building things" into a business empire, focusing on the motorsports and automotive industries.

First profiled in the prestigious Forbes 400 in 1996, Smith has been listed among the wealthiest people in America each year since by the business magazine.

Smith founded Speedway Motorsports, Inc., by consolidating his motorsports holdings in December 1994, and in February 1995 he made it the first motorsports company to trade on the New York Stock Exchange (NYSE:TRK).

Today, Speedway Motorsports owns and operates six premier motorsports facilities: Atlanta Motor Speedway, Bristol Motor Speedway, Las Vegas Motor Speedway, Lowe's Motor Speedway, Infineon Raceway, and Texas Motor Speedway. Speedway Motorsports also provides souvenir-merchandising services through its SMI Properties subsidiary, and manufactures and distributes smaller-scale, modified racing cars through 600 Racing.

O. Bruton Smith is the Chairman of Speedway Motorsports, Inc., and the founder of Speedway Children's Charities.

Smith built his first permanent motorsports facility, Charlotte Motor Speedway, which opened with a 600-mile NASCAR race in June 1960. In 1996, Smith and Speedway Motorsports, Inc., purchased Bristol Motor Speedway from Larry Carrier. As opposed to moving a NASCAR race date away from the .533-mile racing facility as many feared, Smith chose to invest in the venue.

A variety of construction projects, beginning in 1996 and culminating with the opening of the Dale Earnhardt Terrace in 2003, have witnessed Bristol's capacity grow to 160,000. The Speedway boasts more than 150 luxury skybox suites, and its concession, restroom, and other fan amenities are second to none. Smith's vast improvements, coupled with the action-packed racing the concrete oval consistently offers, have established Bristol Motor Speedway as the fans' most popular track that hosts NASCAR sanctioned events. It has been referred to by many as the Lambeau Field of racing. Its events are to motorsports what The Masters is to golf, or what the Kentucky Derby is to horse racing.

We applaud Bruton Smith not only for his outstanding accomplishments and for all he has done to make Bristol Motor Speedway what it is today, but even more so for his sincere willingness and outstanding endeavors to give back to the communities he serves through Speedway Children's Charities. From all of us here at the Junior League of Bristol we say, "Thank you, Bruton Smith."

About Speedway Children's Charities

The Bristol Chapter of Children's Charities was founded in 1996 by Bruton Smith, Chairman of the Board of Speedway Motorsports, Inc., to help children throughout the region surrounding Bristol Motor Speedway. There is a chapter of Speedway Children's Charities at each of Speedway Motorsports' six motorsports facilities.

Operating as a nonprofit foundation, the Bristol Chapter of Speedway Children's Charities is governed by a board of local trustees, whose sole purpose is to distribute the funds raised each year to qualified local children's-based 501c-3 organizations. In that there are no paid employees of the Bristol Chapter, 100 percent of the funds raised are channeled to the agencies. Ms. Claudia H. Byrd, wife of BMS President and General Manager Jeff Byrd, serves as the director of the Bristol Chapter of Speedway Children's Charities.

The major source of funding for Bristol Speedway Children's Charities comes in the form of Speedway in Lights, an annual holiday light display staged on the grounds of Bristol Motor Speedway and Bristol Dragway. More than 250,000 people take the 4.3-mile tour each year. Featuring more than one million lights and over one hundred displays, Speedway in Lights has become a holiday tradition for families throughout the region.

A variety of additional events contributes to the organization's annual proceeds. The Speedway Children's Charities Golf Tournament and the Eastman Motorsports Club Speedway Children's Charities Racing Memorabilia Auction, both held in August, represent major fund-raisers for the organization.

In the first eight years of Bristol Chapter's existence, more than $2.0 million has been distributed to children's-based nonprofit organizations in Northeast Tennessee and Southwest Virginia.

Grant applications are distributed throughout the year and must be submitted prior to June 30 each year. All funds are distributed in November on the opening night of Speedway in Lights. For further information, contact Ms. Claudia Byrd, Director-Bristol Speedway Children's Charities, P. O. Box 3966, Bristol, Tennessee 37625, or call (423) 989-6974.

Rooster in the Hen House

6 eggs
8 drops of A-1 steak sauce
1 ounce milk
Shredded Cheddar cheese (optional)
Chopped cooked ham or other toppings as desired

Combine the eggs, 8 drops of the steak sauce and milk in a bowl. Pour the egg mixture into a lightly buttered pan over medium heat. Stir continuously using a spatula (one bearing SMI logo preferably). Keep the eggs in constant gentle motion; do not allow to stick to the pan. Cook for 6 to 7 minutes or until the desired texture is reached. Fold the cheese and ham into the eggs. Place the eggs in a bowl.

Serves 6

The Grand Bran Cereal Treat

Bran flakes with raisins
Fresh blueberries
1 fresh bran muffin
Skim milk

Fill a medium bowl half full with bran flakes. Add the blueberries and toss to mix. Place the bran muffin in the center of the bowl and break open. Pour milk over the muffin.

Serves 1

Dessert, Anyone?

Please note that this is a delicious complement, and personal favorite, to any entrée, particularly when you can't find the recipe for Cherries Jubilee or Bananas Foster.

One almond nut dark chocolate vanilla ice cream bar

When doing your weekly shopping, stop by the frozen dairy products and pick up a box of ice cream bars. Your choices include dark or light chocolate covering vanilla or chocolate ice cream, with or without nuts. Store in the freezer. When ice cream bars are in your evening dinner menu plans, set your ice cream bars out for 5 to 10 minutes in advance of consumption. This allows the ice cream to soften slightly so as to enhance the experience. When the meal is completed, return to the kitchen and retrieve your awaiting ice cream bar. Gently tear the top of its wrapping and use the paper to wrap around the wooden stick. (For some of you who have discovered you're a little careless with your food, I recommend having an additional paper towel handy.) Enjoy this American delicacy at your leisure (or until the ice cream begins to drip down your hand). Remember there's more in the box if one ice cream bar isn't enough.

Serves 1

A word to dieticians: This particular dessert meets many of the necessary daily food group requirements. DAIRY: ice cream; MEAT: nuts; CHOCOLATE: light or dark.

Introduction

While Bristol may be divided by two states, Tennessee and Virginia, the Twin City is also united by a vibrant sense of community, family, and volunteerism. It is where the birthplace of country music meets the home of the world's fastest half-mile track and the residents share a taste for great cooking and a drive for racing.

This cookbook, *Start Your Ovens: Cooking the Way It Ought'a Be*, grew out of Bristol's love for both, and originates from two of the community's driving forces, the Junior League of Bristol (JLB) and the Bristol Motor Speedway (BMS). *Start Your Ovens* captures the flavor of Bristol, both on the track and in the kitchen. Providing regional favorites from residents and restaurants, plus recipes from NASCAR families such as the Waltrips, the Elliotts, and the Pettys, this book serves as a vehicle for satisfying the appetites of race fans, while filling the needs of the Bristol community.

Fueled by an identical desire to invest in the community, Bristol Motor Speedway and the Junior League of Bristol have been on the forefront of keeping the Bristol community on track. BMS has ignited the economic vitality of the city through enhancements to the track and support of children with Speedway Children's Charities. Keeping the pace, Junior League members have leveraged their momentum through volunteerism, community involvement, and financial commitment to countless community projects for children and families.

Both organizations' roots run deep in the city. For more than half a century, the JLB has been a leader in the fields of education, theatre, cultural arts, health care, and community and economic development. Shifting gears during times of change, members have brought great energy to projects that provide affordable childcare and free dental care to indigent families, or help provide children with a haven from domestic abuse or a safe place to play in community parks.

Bristol Motor Speedway has made Bristol attractive for recreation for all ages as fans' favorite pit stop along the NASCAR Winston Cup and Busch Series circuit. Located on a former dairy farm and once recognized as Bristol International Raceway, the shape and scope of today's Bristol Motor Speedway materialized from rough sketches on envelopes and paper bags. Striving for an intimate setting, founders chose to establish a half-mile facility rather than the originally surveyed 1.5-mile track in Charlotte, North Carolina.

This recipe for success worked. Bristol's very first NASCAR race, held on July 30, 1961, drew an audience of 18,000 spectators. Today, the number of race fans has increased sevenfold and the facility has evolved into the largest sports arena in Tennessee. Twice a year, Bristol becomes a kaleidoscope, with a steady procession of spectators sporting their drivers' colors and numbers. Flags, ball caps, T-shirts, stickers, and sunglasses are standard attire, serving to boast the fans' favorites. Waiting to cash in on this fervor, souvenir trucks run the length of the track with a complete lineup of die-cast replica cars, scaled-down helmets, license plates, radios, jackets, and other keepsakes, even shards of the inevitable wrecks.

Although Bristol's entire population could wrap around the oval concrete track three times, Bristol Motor Speedway's growing seating capacity of 160,000 is still not large enough to accommodate the influx of fans. BMS has become the hottest ticket on the circuit, with seats not the only thing in short supply. Accommodations are a hot commodity. Following the usual roulette of hotel rooms, a small city goes up around the racetrack as fans set up residence. Shelters range from makeshift tents to luxury motor homes lining the approach to the stands. Meanwhile, other fans bunk with locals who rent their homes, extra bedrooms, or backyards.

Sandwiched between weekend neighbors from fifty states, the Middle and Far East, Western Europe, and even "Down Under," die-hard fans feel right at home. Individuals who sometimes have nothing else in common seem to be both allied by their mutual love for the sport and divided by their loyalty to a single driver.

From the green to checkered flag, the grandstands, rippling in a sea of local residents and visitors, come alive with a deafening roar of horse and lung power. Bristol Motor Speedway is banked 36 degrees in the corners and 16 degrees in the straightaways, often causing some degree of pandemonium. It is no surprise that this short track stages one of the most exciting events during the race season, prompting a flurry of caution flags as drivers get passed by, swept up, and spun around, their cars casualties of the "Bristol Bump."

From our region to the racetrack to your kitchen, the Junior League of Bristol, with the support of the Bristol Motor Speedway and the Winston Cup Racing Wives Auxiliary, is proud to present to you this snapshot of our local flavor for racing and recipes.

Members of the Junior League of Bristol

extend our gratitude to

Diane Hough and Renee Zaremski of

the Winston Cup Racing Wives Auxiliary

for their support of this cookbook.

We also thank the drivers' wives and family members

who submitted recipes, including

Nancy Andretti, Debbie Benson, Lynn Bodine,

Meredith Bowman, Cindy Elliott,

Diane Green, Linda Helton,

Arlene Martin, Ginny McClure, Lynda Petty,

Pattie Petty, Ann Schrader,

Elizabeth "Buffy" Waltrip, and Nancy Wood.

Table of Contents

The History of the Junior League of Bristol

In a decade when Americans were serving their country in war, volunteers of the Junior League of Bristol (JLB) were serving their communities with the same vigor and duty. In 1948, the Junior League of Bristol, formerly recognized as the League Border Guild, was chartered. Since then, it has inspired more than fifty years of community service in an ever-changing society.

In an age of poodle skirts and penny loafers, the JLB made its own fashion statement through the Bargain Box, a community thrift shop, where all walks of life could sport the same styles of shoes. Meanwhile, profits from the shop made cultural arts and education more fashionable to the community through programs supported by the League. These programs exposed all ages to art, drama, and music, and inspired children with tall tales and literary facts during story time at the public library.

As the sixties shrieked with sounds of rock and roll, the Junior League of Bristol stayed in tune with the community's needs. Members brought music to the ears of young and old through their support of symphony youth concerts and the Bristol Speech and Hearing Center. The League also endorsed an art education program for elementary schools and a record, print, and sculpture collection for the local library. Serving as a cornerstone for several community programs, the League made monetary donations to building funds for the YMCA and Mental Health Center.

Although the seventies saw the dawn of an international energy crisis, the League never lost its power. Members had a hand in igniting a variety of programs that enhanced the quality of life for others. The organization financed six months' use of a Xeroradiography machine for Bristol Memorial Hospital and sponsored a public education program on breast self-examination. Members also contributed monetary donations to the Bristol Life Saving Crew, hospital nursery, and Salvation Army.

In the 1980s, women achieved new heights in the workplace, from Sally Ride as the first woman to travel into space to League member Sandra Day O'Connor as the first woman to sit on the Supreme Court. As JLB became more diverse, members used their experience and expertise to strengthen communities through shared solutions. In addition to founding a community volunteer program, JLB supported Bristol's restoration of the historic Paramount Theatre and the revitalization of Steele Creek Park. With a hunger to satisfy greater challenges, members participated in the community's first annual food drive.

Technology exploded in the nineties, creating a community that relied on modems, cell phones, and voice mail for communication. The League never lost its personal touch, donating funds to the Children's Advocacy Center so a child's voice could still be heard. As more families entered the workforce and affordable, quality childcare became less abundant, the League contributed financial resources toward the development of the Building Blocks Day Care Center to offer families sliding-scale fees. Recognizing the value of an education, members granted support to the Virginia High Day Care Center so young mothers could meet the challenges of modern society by staying in school.

As time has passed, so has the world changed with the new millennium. Yet, in the midst of this rapid change, the Junior League of Bristol has remained the same. Continuing to make the community a more vital place to live and grow, members have helped provide dental care for the working uninsured, a safe haven for child victims of domestic abuse, and a safe place for children to play.

Over the years, the Junior League's style has been tailored to mirror more fashionable days and its programs have been altered to echo the times. The League's legacy, however, has remained the same, enhancing the economic, educational, cultural, and civic conditions of the community through volunteerism and community service.

Original Start Your Ovens Committee

Chairmen

Susan Key-Higinbothom • Donna Green Sikorski

Committee Members

Landy Adams • Zanna Blankenbeckler • Tracey Bowers

Kimberly Bradley • Edie Cannon • Paula Countiss

Rita Estes • Molly Fox • Catherine Haynes • Amy Mathes

Jennifer McQueary • Karen McSharry

Christine Mullins • Dianna Mullins • Karen Pennington

Suzanne Senter • Kristina Willis

Cookbook Chairmen

1999–2002 Susan Key-Higinbothom • Donna Green Sikorski

2002–2003 Susan Key-Higinbothom • Molly Fox

2003–2004 Amy Shuttle

2004–2005 Melinda Upchurch

2005–2006 Lynn Couch

Cookbook Executive Liaison

2003–2006 Susan Key-Higinbothom

Hello Friends,

I got my first taste of speed in a go-cart at age twelve, and, since then, have given 100 percent to God, my family, and racing.

I enjoyed a terrific driving career behind the wheel of cars owned by some of NASCAR's best car owners, won a lot of races, three championships, and the Daytona 500. When I look back on my favorite moments in racing, Bristol always stands out. I won twelve NASCAR Winston Cup races at Bristol, and my streak of seven-straight victories at Bristol is one of my proudest achievements. Bruton even named a grandstand for ol' D. W., so Bristol truly holds a special place in my heart.

A lot changed for this city over the years, as the track and its grandstands grew to accommodate and serve the racing community. Keeping the pace in community service, the Junior League of Bristol made its own mark on Bristol as a driving force in volunteerism and community service.

Now the Junior League of Bristol presents another vehicle for raising funds to meet the needs of the community. This new cookbook, *Start Your Ovens: Cooking the Way It Ought'a Be,* gives you a real taste of Bristol. The recipes blend local flavor with some favorites served to well-known NASCAR families. Whether you're a seasoned race fan or a cook with seasoned taste, your purchase of this book will help fuel the League's efforts to build a stronger community for children and families.

Sincerely,

Darrell Waltrip

Menus
Start Your Ovens

Night Race Tailgate Supper

Thunder Valley Frozen Margaritas

Black Bean Mango Salsa with tortilla chips

Picnic Sandwiches for a Crowd

Broccoli Salad Supreme

Checkered Flag Brownies

Sky Box VIP Lunch

Marinated Roast Beef Tenderloin with prepared
horseradish and mayonnaise

Potato Refrigerator Rolls

Boiled peel 'n' eat shrimp with cocktail sauce

Parrish's Salad

Super Chocolate Chip Cookies

Supper on the Lake

Splash 'n' Go Punch

Tomato Basil Hummus with sesame crackers

Grilled Teriyaki Chicken Salad

Crusty rolls

Butter Brickle Bars

Mountain Empire Gourmet Dinner

Super Speedy Stuffed Mushrooms

Chilled Cantaloupe and Champagne Soup

Patagonian Potato-Encrusted Trout

Lemon Couscous

Chilled Asparagus with Herbed Yogurt Sauce

Short-Track Blackberry Shortcake

Spring Race Barbecue Supper

Assorted beer and soft drinks

Baked Mexicorn Dip with corn chips

Bristol Slow-Cooker Barbecue on sesame buns

Classic Creamy Coleslaw

Best Times Baked Beans

Victory Kisses

Almost Fat-Free Banana Pudding

Fourth-of-July Grill Party

Tequila Sunset Punch

Greek Feta Dip with Pita Points

High-Octane Tomatoes

Spicy Grilled Shrimp

Grilled Steaks with Ancho Chile Lime Butter

Favorite Red Potato Salad

Grilled Corn

French bread

Oreo Ice Cream Cake

Autumn Harvest Supper

Baked Spinach Dip with crackers

Autumn Pork Chops

Confetti-Stuffed Acorn Squash

Baked Mushroom Rice

Pumpkin Pie Crumb Cake

Holiday Open House

Hot Mulled Cranberry Punch

Cosmo Punch

Sesame Pork Tenderloin with Dipping Sauce

Onion Soufflé Dip with wheat crackers

Layered Artichoke Torta with crackers

Nutty Cheese Bruschetta

Famous Salmon Roll with crackers

Sweet Potato Pecan Bread

Praline Crunch

Christmas Crescents

South-of-the-Border Supper Party

Sangria

Southern Caviar with chips

Spinach Salad with Poppy Seed Dressing

Fast-Track Fiesta Chicken Bake

White rice

Shoe Peg corn with butter

Angel Food Cake with
fresh strawberries and whipped cream

Bridal Luncheon

Ruby Royale

State Street Tomato Bisque

Tullamore Greens

Shrimp in Champagne Sauce
with Pasta

Roasted Asparagus

Strawberries Romanoff

Drivers' Wives Bristol Luncheon 2000

Sweet iced tea

Cheese Straws

Orzo Artichoke Salad

Tropical Chicken Salad on croissants

Fresh fruit medley

Chocolate Pound Cake with Peanut Butter Frosting

Almond Cake with Raspberry Sauce

"Start Your Ovens" Cover Menu

Thunder Valley Frozen Margaritas

Jamaican Corn

Race Weekend Kabobs with
Louisiana Marinade

Happy
Hour

Appetizers & Beverages

Marinated Roast Beef Tenderloin

Coarsely ground black pepper or
   lemon pepper seasoning to taste
1 (5- to 8-pound) beef tenderloin,
   trimmed
1½ to 2 cups soy sauce
½ to ¾ cup bourbon
2 garlic cloves, crushed
3 or 4 slices bacon
1 medium onion, sliced

Sprinkle the pepper over the surface of the tenderloin. Place the tenderloin in a sealable plastic bag. Pour a mixture of the soy sauce, bourbon and garlic over the tenderloin and seal tightly. Marinate at room temperature for 2 hours or in the refrigerator for 8 to 10 hours, turning occasionally.

Bring the tenderloin to room temperature if refrigerated. Drain, reserving the marinade. Place the tenderloin on a rack in a roasting pan; tuck the ends under. Arrange the bacon over the top and drizzle with the reserved marinade. Top with the sliced onion.

Place the tenderloin in a preheated 450-degree oven. Reduce the oven temperature to 400 degrees. Roast for 30 to 50 minutes or until of the desired degree of doneness. A meat thermometer should register 145 degrees for medium-rare.

Yield: *25 servings*

Famous Salmon Roll

1 (14-ounce) can salmon, drained
8 ounces cream cheese, softened
1 tablespoon lemon juice
2 teaspoons minced onion
1 teaspoon horseradish
1 cup chopped fresh parsley
3/4 cup chopped pecans

Combine the salmon, cream cheese, lemon juice, onion and horseradish in a bowl and mix well. Shape the salmon mixture into a loaf. Roll in the parsley and pecans. Chill, wrapped in plastic wrap, until serving time. Serve with assorted party crackers. May prepare several days in advance and store, covered, in the refrigerator. Reduce the fat grams by substituting reduced-fat cream cheese for the cream cheese.

Yield: *10 servings*

Spicy Grilled Shrimp

1/2 cup soy sauce
1/2 cup olive oil
5 tablespoons Cajun seasoning
1/4 cup sesame oil
1/4 cup lemon juice
2 tablespoons minced gingerroot
2 teaspoons dry mustard
2 teaspoons hot pepper sauce
32 large shrimp, peeled, deveined

Combine the soy sauce, olive oil, Cajun seasoning, sesame oil, lemon juice, gingerroot, dry mustard and hot pepper sauce in a bowl and mix well. Pour over the shrimp in a sealable plastic bag. Seal tightly.

Marinate at room temperature for 30 minutes, turning once or twice. Drain, discarding the marinade. Place the shrimp in an oiled grill basket. Grill over direct heat for 1 to 3 minutes per side or until the shrimp turn pink.

Yield: *8 servings*

Pacific Rim Shrimp Tostadas

Serve with a Mexican or Asian entrée.

9 (6-inch) corn tortillas
3 unpeeled garlic cloves
2 teaspoons cumin
1½ pounds medium shrimp, peeled,
    deveined
3½ teaspoons finely grated lime zest
6 tablespoons lime juice
6 tablespoons nonfat yogurt
6 tablespoons chopped fresh cilantro
2½ teaspoons minced seeded
    jalapeño chile
Salt and pepper to taste

Cut each tortilla into 6 wedges. Arrange the wedges in a single layer on 2 large baking sheets. Bake at 325 degrees for 30 minutes or until crisp, turning once.

Spray a small baking dish with nonstick cooking spray. Add the garlic. Roast, covered with foil, for 30 minutes or until tender. Let stand until cool. Peel the garlic and mash in a bowl. Stir in the cumin.

Bring enough water to cover the shrimp generously to a boil in a stockpot. Add the shrimp and lime zest. Cook for 3 minutes or until the shrimp turn pink. Drain through a fine strainer, reserving the shrimp and lime zest. Let stand until cool.

Chop the shrimp coarsely. Combine the shrimp, reserved lime zest, lime juice, yogurt, cilantro, jalapeño chile and garlic mixture in a bowl and mix well. Season with salt and pepper. Spoon the shrimp mixture onto the tortilla wedges. Arrange on a serving platter. Serve immediately.

Yield: *18 servings*

Nutty Cheese Bruschetta

½ cup freshly grated Parmesan
    cheese
¼ cup chopped walnuts
¼ teaspoon salt
¼ cup olive oil
½ loaf French bread
Olive oil to taste
¼ cup freshly grated Parmesan
    cheese
¼ cup chopped walnuts

Combine ½ cup cheese, ¼ cup walnuts and salt in a food processor container. Pulse until the walnuts are finely chopped. Add ¼ cup olive oil. Process until smooth.

Cut the bread diagonally into ½-inch slices. Spray both sides of the slices lightly with olive oil to taste or nonstick olive oil cooking spray. Arrange the slices in a single layer on a baking sheet. Broil 6 inches from the heat source for 30 seconds on each side or until brown, turning once.

Spread each slice with some of the cheese mixture. Sprinkle with ¼ cup cheese and press ¼ cup walnuts over the top. Broil for 30 to 40 seconds or until the cheese begins to melt.

Yield: *20 to 30 servings*

Bristol Motor Speedway could very easily have opened in 1961 under a different name. The first proposed site for the speedway was in Piney Flats but, according to Carl Moore, who built the track along with Larry Carrier and R. G. Pope, the idea met local opposition. So the track that could have been called Piney Flats International Speedway was built five miles down the road on 11-E in Bristol.

23

Tomato, Pepper and Goat Cheese Bruschetta

6 to 8 plum tomatoes, chopped
1 roasted red or yellow bell pepper,
    chopped (optional)
1 tablespoon olive oil
1½ teaspoons onion salt
6 to 8 fresh basil leaves, chopped
½ loaf crusty Italian bread
½ cup (1 stick) butter, softened
Garlic salt to taste
3 ounces goat cheese

Combine the tomatoes, bell pepper, olive oil, onion salt and basil in a bowl and mix well. Marinate at room temperature for 30 minutes or longer, stirring occasionally.

Cut the bread into ½-inch slices. Spread with the butter and sprinkle with garlic salt. Arrange the slices in a single layer on a baking sheet.

Broil for 20 to 30 seconds per side or until light brown; watch closely. Spread the goat cheese on the warm slices. Spoon some of the tomato mixture on each slice. Arrange on a serving platter. Serve immediately.

Yield: *20 to 25 servings*

Pesto Pinwheels

For a homemade pesto recipe, see page 155.

1 sheet frozen puff pastry
1/3 cup pesto
1/2 cup grated Parmesan cheese
1 egg
1 teaspoon water

Thaw the pastry using package directions. Unfold the pastry. Roll into an 11×14-inch rectangle on a lightly floured surface. Spread with the pesto and sprinkle with the cheese. Roll as for a jelly roll.

Cut the roll into 3/8-inch slices. Arrange the slices cut side up on a lightly greased baking sheet. Brush each slice with a mixture of the egg and water. Bake at 400 degrees for 8 to 10 minutes or until golden brown. Remove to a serving platter. Serve warm.

Yield: *35 pinwheels*

Tortilla Pinwheels

8 ounces cream cheese, softened
2 teaspoons milk
1/8 teaspoon garlic powder
1 (4-ounce) can diced green chiles, drained
1/2 cup chopped seeded tomato
1 tablespoon minced onion
1/8 teaspoon salt
4 (9-inch) flour tortillas

Combine the cream cheese, milk and garlic powder in a mixing bowl. Beat until light and fluffy. Stir in the green chiles, tomato, onion and salt. Moisten both sides of the tortillas lightly with water. Spread 3 tablespoons of the cream cheese mixture on 1 side of each tortilla. Roll tightly to enclose the filling. Wrap each roll individually in plastic wrap. Freeze for 30 minutes. Transfer the rolls to the refrigerator. Trim 1/2 inch from the ends of each roll. Cut the rolls into 1/2-inch slices. Arrange the pinwheels on a serving platter. Serve immediately.

Yield: *32 pinwheels*

Super Speedy Stuffed Mushrooms

Pattie Petty, wife of Kyle Petty

Medium white mushrooms
2 tablespoons butter, melted
1/4 cup (1/2 stick) butter
3 tablespoons shredded Monterey
    Jack cheese
1 garlic clove, minced
1/3 cup fine whole wheat saltine
    crumbs
2 tablespoons dry white wine
1 teaspoon soy sauce
3 tablespoons grated Parmesan
    cheese

Rinse and dry the mushrooms. Remove the stems and discard. Brush the mushroom caps with 2 tablespoons melted butter. Combine 1/4 cup butter, Monterey Jack cheese and garlic in a bowl and mix well. Stir in the cracker crumbs, wine and soy sauce.

Arrange the mushroom caps cavity side up on a baking sheet with sides. Fill the caps with the butter mixture and press lightly. Sprinkle with the Parmesan cheese. Broil 6 inches from the heat source for 3 minutes or until light brown. Serve immediately.

Yield: *variable*

High-Octane Tomatoes

These tomatoes will be the hit of your next cocktail party.

60 grape tomatoes
1 tablespoon kosher salt, or to taste
Vodka

Remove the stems from the tomatoes. Place the tomatoes in a sealable plastic bag. Add the salt. Pour enough vodka over the tomatoes to cover. Seal tightly. Marinate for 8 to 10 hours, turning occasionally; drain. Serve in a glass or silver bowl with wooden picks.

Yield: *20 servings*

Cheese Straws

This snack was served at the 2000 Drivers' Wives Luncheon.

8 ounces extra-sharp Cheddar cheese,
    shredded
½ cup (1 stick) butter, softened
1 tablespoon Tabasco sauce
½ teaspoon salt
⅛ to ¼ teaspoon cayenne pepper
1½ cups flour
Paprika to taste
Salt to taste

Combine the cheese, butter, Tabasco sauce, ½ teaspoon salt and cayenne pepper in a bowl and mix well. Add the flour, stirring until a soft and easily handled dough forms. Spoon the dough into a cookie press fitted with #1 disc or small star disc. Press into long strips on an ungreased shiny baking sheet.

Bake at 350 degrees for 20 minutes. Cut the warm strips into 2-inch pieces. Cool on the baking sheet. Sprinkle lightly with paprika and salt to taste. Store in an airtight container. If a cookie press is not available, roll the dough on a lightly floured surface and cut into strips.

Yield: *6 dozen cheese straws*

The land that Bristol Motor Speedway is built on used to be a dairy farm.

Baked Artichoke Dip

2 cups shredded Cheddar cheese
1 (14-ounce) can artichoke hearts,
    drained, chopped
1 (6-ounce) jar marinated artichoke
    hearts, drained, chopped
1 (4-ounce) can diced green chiles,
    drained
6 tablespoons mayonnaise

Combine the cheese, artichokes and green chiles in a bowl and mix well. Stir in the mayonnaise. Spoon the artichoke mixture into a 1½-quart baking dish sprayed with nonstick cooking spray. Bake at 350 degrees for 20 minutes. Serve warm with corn chips or assorted party crackers.

Yield: *8 to 10 servings*

Black Bean Mango Salsa

1 (15-ounce) can black beans,
    drained, rinsed
1 (14-ounce) can white corn, drained
2 mangoes, chopped
½ cup finely chopped red onion
½ red bell pepper, chopped
½ yellow bell pepper, chopped
¼ cup finely chopped cilantro
1 envelope ranch salad dressing mix
Salt and pepper to taste

Combine the beans, corn, mangoes, onion, bell peppers and cilantro in a bowl and mix well. Add the dressing mix and mix well. Season with salt and pepper. Marinate, covered, at room temperature for 3 hours, stirring occasionally. Serve with tortilla chips or large corn chips.

Yield: *12 to 15 servings*

Hot Clam Dip

1 medium yellow onion,
    finely chopped
$^1/_2$ cup (1 stick) butter
2 (6-ounce) cans minced clams
1 cup Italian bread crumbs
1 teaspoon oregano
1 teaspoon parsley flakes
1 teaspoon lemon juice
2 drops of Tabasco sauce
2 cups shredded extra-sharp
    Cheddar cheese

Sauté the onion in the butter in a skillet until tender. Combine the undrained clams, bread crumbs, oregano, parsley flakes, lemon juice and Tabasco sauce in a bowl and mix well. Stir in the onion.

Spoon the clam mixture into a 9-inch round baking pan sprayed with nonstick cooking spray. Sprinkle with the cheese. Bake at 350 degrees for 20 minutes or until brown and bubbly. Serve hot with assorted party crackers.

Yield: *10 to 12 servings*

Hot Crab Meat Dip

8 ounces cream cheese, softened
1 tablespoon milk
2 (6-ounce) cans crab meat, drained
3 tablespoons chopped green onions
1 to 2 tablespoons lemon juice, or
    to taste
1 tablespoon horseradish, or to taste
$^1/_4$ teaspoon Tabasco sauce, or to taste
$^1/_8$ teaspoon seasoned salt
$^1/_8$ teaspoon seasoned pepper
$^1/_2$ cup slivered almonds
Parsley flakes

Combine the cream cheese and milk in a bowl and mix well. Stir in the crab meat, green onions, lemon juice, horseradish, Tabasco sauce, seasoned salt and seasoned pepper. Spoon the crab meat mixture into a 1-quart baking dish sprayed with nonstick cooking spray. Sprinkle with the almonds and parsley flakes.

Bake at 375 degrees for 25 minutes. Serve hot with melba rounds. May be prepared in advance and stored, covered, in the refrigerator until just before baking. Sprinkle with the almonds and parsley just before baking.

Yield: *10 to 15 servings*

Greek Feta Dip with Pita Points

16 ounces feta cheese, crumbled
3 or 4 plum tomatoes, chopped
3 or 4 green onions, chopped
10 to 12 kalamata olives, chopped
2 tablespoons olive oil
1 garlic clove, chopped
½ package pita rounds
Garlic salt to taste

Combine the feta cheese, tomatoes, green onions, olives, olive oil and chopped garlic in a bowl and mix well.

Separate the pita rounds. Cut each round into wedges. Arrange the wedges in a single layer on a baking sheet. Sprinkle with garlic salt. Broil until brown and crisp. Serve with the feta dip.

Yield: *20 to 25 servings*

Onion Soufflé Dip

24 ounces cream cheese, softened
2 cups shredded fresh Parmesan
    cheese
½ cup mayonnaise
12 to 16 ounces frozen chopped
    onions, thawed, drained
Paprika

Combine the cream cheese, Parmesan cheese and mayonnaise in a bowl and mix well. Stir in the onions. Spoon into a baking dish sprayed with nonstick cooking spray. Sprinkle with paprika. Bake at 425 degrees for 20 to 30 minutes or until brown and bubbly. Serve hot with bagel chips or corn chips.

Yield: *25 to 30 servings*

Baked Spinach Dip

8 ounces Monterey Jack cheese,
    shredded
8 ounces cream cheese, softened
1½ (10-ounce) packages frozen
    chopped spinach, thawed,
    drained
1 (14-ounce) can diced tomatoes
¾ cup chopped onion
⅓ cup half-and-half
1 to 2 tablespoons chopped seeded
    jalapeño chiles
Garlic salt to taste

Combine the Monterey Jack cheese, cream
cheese, spinach, undrained tomatoes, onion,
half-and-half, jalapeño chiles and garlic salt in a
bowl and mix well. Spoon the spinach mixture
into a buttered 7×10-inch baking dish. Bake at
400 degrees for 20 to 25 minutes or until bubbly.
Serve hot with pita crisps or wheat crackers.

Yield: *10 to 12 servings*

Baked Mexicorn Dip

2 (11-ounce) cans Mexican-style
    corn
1 cup shredded Monterey Jack
    cheese
1 (4-ounce) can mild green chiles,
    drained
1 (4-ounce) jar diced pimentos,
    drained
1 cup mayonnaise

Combine the corn, cheese, green chiles and
pimentos in a bowl and mix well. Stir in the
mayonnaise. Spoon the corn mixture into a
round baking dish sprayed with nonstick cooking
spray. Bake at 325 degrees for 30 to 45 minutes
or until bubbly. Serve hot with corn chips.

Yield: *8 to 10 servings*

Night Race Nacho Dip

This is a great race-watching snack.

8 ounces cream cheese, softened
1 (15-ounce) can chili with beans, or
    1½ to 2 cups homemade chili
1 (4-ounce) can chopped green chiles,
    drained
2 tablespoons chopped seeded
    jalapeño chiles
1 bunch green onions, chopped
2 cups shredded Cheddar or
    Monterey Jack cheese, or a
    combination

Layer the cream cheese, chili, green chiles, jalapeño chiles, green onions and cheese in the order listed in a 7×10-inch or round baking dish sprayed with nonstick cooking spray. Bake for 30 minutes or until bubbly. Serve hot with corn chips or tortilla chips.

Yield: *10 to 12 servings*

Seating capacity for the very first NASCAR race at BMS—held on July 30, 1961—was 18,000. Prior to this race, the speedway hosted weekly races.

Southwestern Caponata

1 tablespoon pine nuts
2 tablespoons olive oil
2 cups (1-inch-cubes) peeled eggplant
1/2 cup chopped yellow onion
1/2 cup chopped yellow bell pepper
1/2 cup chopped green bell pepper
1/2 cup chopped red bell pepper
2 tablespoons olive oil
1 cup canned diced tomatoes
4 teaspoons chopped fresh parsley
1 tablespoon red wine vinegar
2 teaspoons minced seeded
    jalapeño chile
2 teaspoons drained rinsed capers
1/2 teaspoon minced garlic
1/8 teaspoon sugar
1/8 teaspoon salt
4 ounces goat cheese, crumbled
1/2 cup (1 stick) butter, softened
1 loaf French bread, cut into
    1/2-inch slices

Place the pine nuts in a small baking pan. Toast at 350 degrees for 5 minutes or until light brown. Heat 2 tablespoons olive oil in a sauté pan over medium heat. Add the eggplant. Sauté for 15 minutes. Stir in the onion, bell peppers, 2 tablespoons olive oil, tomatoes, parsley, wine vinegar, jalapeño chile, capers, garlic, sugar, salt and pine nuts.

Simmer over low heat for 30 minutes, stirring occasionally. Spoon the eggplant mixture into an 8×8-inch baking dish sprayed with nonstick cooking spray. Sprinkle with the goat cheese. Bake at 350 degrees for 30 minutes.

Spread the butter on both sides of the bread slices. Arrange the slices on a baking sheet. Toast until brown on both sides, turning once. Serve with the caponata.

Yield: *8 to 10 servings*

Southern Caviar

Serve in a sterilized terra-cotta flowerpot.

1 (15-ounce) can chick-peas, drained,
    rinsed
1 (14-ounce) can black-eyed peas,
    drained, rinsed
1 (14-ounce) can black beans,
    drained, rinsed
2 medium tomatoes, chopped
1 medium red bell pepper, chopped
1/2 cup chopped onion
1/2 cup chopped fresh parsley or
    cilantro
1 jalapeño chile, seeded, chopped
4 green onions, chopped
2 garlic cloves, crushed
1 (8-ounce) bottle Italian salad
    dressing

Combine the chick-peas, black-eyed peas, black beans, tomatoes, bell pepper, onion, parsley, jalapeño chile, green onions and garlic in a bowl and mix gently. Add the salad dressing and toss to coat. Chill, covered, for 2 to 10 hours, stirring occasionally; drain. Serve with tortilla chips.

Yield: *12 to 15 servings*

Tomato Basil Hummus

1 (15-ounce) can garbanzos
1/4 cup tahini
Juice of 1 lemon
2 tablespoons olive oil
1 garlic clove, chopped
1/2 teaspoon salt
2 or 3 Roma tomatoes, chopped
6 to 8 fresh basil leaves, chopped
Salt and pepper to taste

Drain the beans, reserving 1/4 cup of the liquid. Combine the beans, reserved liquid, tahini, lemon juice, olive oil, garlic and 1/2 teaspoon salt in a food processor container. Process until smooth. Spread the garbanzo mixture on a small platter.

Combine the tomatoes and basil in a bowl and mix gently. Add salt and pepper to taste. Sprinkle over the prepared layer. Serve with toasted pita wedges.

Yield: *4 to 6 servings*

Layered Artichoke Torta

16 ounces cream cheese, softened
1 envelope ranch salad dressing mix
1 (6-ounce) jar marinated artichoke
    hearts, drained, chopped
1/3 cup chopped drained roasted
    red peppers
3 tablespoons minced fresh parsley

Combine the cream cheese and dressing mix in a bowl and mix well. Combine the artichokes, roasted peppers and parsley in a bowl and mix well.

Line a 3-cup mold with plastic wrap. Alternate layers of the cream cheese mixture and artichoke mixture in the prepared mold until all of the ingredients are used, beginning and ending with the cream cheese mixture. Chill, covered, for 8 to 10 hours. Invert onto a serving platter; discard the plastic wrap. Serve with assorted party crackers.

Yield: *10 to 12 servings*

Off the Wall Cheese Ball

8 ounces cream cheese, softened
1/4 cup grated Parmesan cheese
1/4 cup chopped pimento-stuffed
    green olives
1 (3-ounce) package dried
    chipped beef
2 teaspoons prepared horseradish
2 teaspoons Worcestershire sauce
2 cups crushed potato chips

Combine the cream cheese and Parmesan cheese in a bowl and mix well. Stir in the olives, chipped beef, horseradish and Worcestershire sauce. Shape the cream cheese mixture into a ball. Roll in the potato chips. Chill, covered, until serving time. Serve with assorted party crackers.

Yield: *10 to 12 servings*

Sherry Cheese Spread

8 ounces cream cheese, softened
1 cup shredded sharp Cheddar
    cheese
4 teaspoons sherry
1/2 teaspoon curry powder
1 (8-ounce) jar chutney
3 or 4 green onions with tops,
    finely sliced

Combine the cream cheese, Cheddar cheese, sherry and curry powder in a bowl and mix well. Spread the cream cheese mixture 1/2 inch thick on a serving platter. Chill, covered, for 30 to 60 minutes. Spread with the chutney. Sprinkle with the green onions. Serve with assorted party crackers.

Yield: *8 to 10 servings*

Shrimp Cocktail Spread

1 (3-ounce) package lemon gelatin
1/2 cup hot water
1 (10-ounce) can tomato soup
8 ounces cream cheese, cubed
1/2 cup mayonnaise-type salad
    dressing
2 (4-ounce) cans cocktail shrimp,
    drained
1/2 cup finely chopped onion
1/2 cup chopped celery
1/8 teaspoon Worcestershire sauce
Peeled steamed shrimp with tails

Dissolve the gelatin in the hot water and stir. Bring the soup to a boil in a saucepan. Add the gelatin mixture, cream cheese and salad dressing to the soup. Spoon the soup mixture into a mixing bowl. Beat until blended. Let stand until cool. Stir in the canned shrimp, onion, celery and Worcestershire sauce. Spoon the shrimp mixture into a mold. Chill, covered, for 8 hours or until set. Invert onto a serving platter. Garnish with steamed shrimp. Serve with assorted party crackers.

Yield: *10 to 12 servings*

Ruby Royale

3/4 cup thawed cranberry juice
    cocktail concentrate
1/4 cup cranberry or raspberry
    liqueur
1/4 cup orange liqueur
1 bottle Champagne or other
    sparkling wine, chilled
6 orange slices
12 fresh cranberries

Combine 2 tablespoons of the cranberry juice cocktail concentrate, 2 teaspoons of the cranberry liqueur and 2 teaspoons of the orange liqueur in each of 6 Champagne flutes. Add enough Champagne to fill the flutes and stir gently. Garnish each serving with an orange slice and 2 cranberries skewered on a wooden pick.

Yield: *6 servings*

Sangria

2 (750-milliliter) bottles dry red wine,
    chilled
1 cup lemon juice
1 cup orange juice
1 cup sugar
2 small lemons, sliced, seeded
2 small oranges, sliced, seeded
Orange juice ice cubes
2 (1-quart) bottles club soda or
    ginger ale (optional)

Combine the wine, lemon juice, orange juice and sugar in a 6-quart container and stir until the sugar dissolves. Add the lemon slices and orange slices and mix well. Chill, covered, until serving time. Pour the sangria over orange juice ice cubes in glasses, adding club soda to dilute if desired.

Yield: *10 to 12 servings*

Thunder Valley Frozen Margaritas

The photo for this recipe appears on the front cover.

1 (1.5 liter) bottle tequila
4 quarts water
2 cups Triple Sec
4 (12-ounce) cans frozen limeade
    concentrate, thawed
2 (10-ounce) cans frozen
    margarita mix
Lime juice
Coarse salt

Combine the tequila, water, Triple Sec, limeade concentrate and margarita mix in a large plastic container and mix well. Freeze for 48 hours; the mixture will freeze to a slushy consistency. Moisten the rims of margarita glasses with lime juice and coat the rims with coarse salt. Fill each glass with the slushy margarita mixture.

Yield: *15 to 20 servings*

Banana Slush Punch

3 quarts water
8 cups pineapple juice
8 cups sugar
5 cups orange juice
1 cup lemon juice
10 medium bananas, mashed
2¹/₂ (2-liter) bottles lemon-lime soda,
    chilled

Combine the water, pineapple juice, sugar, orange juice and lemon juice in a large container and mix well. Stir in the bananas. Freeze, covered, until ready to serve. Thaw to a slushy consistency. Pour into a punch bowl. Add the soda and mix well. Ladle into punch cups.

To make smaller batches, divide the fruit mixture into 5 equal portions and freeze. Add ¹/₂ of a 2-liter bottle of lemon-lime soda to each batch.

Yield: *100 (1-cup) servings*

Cosmo Punch

Great summertime beverage—smooth and light.

2 cups vodka
1 cup Triple Sec
Juice of 3 limes
1 (64-ounce) bottle cranberry
    juice cocktail

Combine the vodka, Triple Sec, lime juice and cranberry juice cocktail in a large container. Pour over ice in glasses. May pour the punch over an ice ring or ice cubes made of cranberry juice in a punch bowl.

Yield: 15 (³⁄₄-cup) servings

Creamy Pineapple Punch

1 (46-ounce) can pineapple juice,
    chilled
1¹⁄₂ pints vanilla ice cream, softened
1 pint orange sherbet, softened
3 cups ginger ale, chilled

Combine the pineapple juice, ice cream and sherbet in a punch bowl and stir until blended. Add the ginger ale and mix well. Ladle into punch cups.

Yield: 18 (³⁄₄-cup) servings

Tequila Sunset Punch

1⅓ cups sugar
1 cup water
¼ cup grenadine
2 (750-milliliter) bottles dry
    white wine
1 cup tequila
½ cup Triple Sec
½ cup orange juice
½ cup lime juice
Seltzer (optional)
1 orange, thinly sliced
2 limes, thinly sliced

Combine the sugar and water in a saucepan. Heat over medium-high heat until the sugar dissolves, stirring frequently. Pour ⅔ cup of the sugar syrup into a heatproof 1-quart glass measuring cup. Stir in the grenadine. Add enough water to measure 1 quart. Pour into 2 ice cube trays. Freeze for 24 hours.

Combine the remaining sugar syrup, wine, tequila, Triple Sec, orange juice and lime juice in a 1-gallon pitcher. Chill, covered, in the refrigerator for 24 hours. Add the grenadine ice cubes to the punch just before serving. Pour into individual glasses as is, or add a splash of seltzer. Garnish each serving with orange and lime slices.

Yield: *12 servings*

The first driver on the track for practice on July 27, 1961, was Tiny Lund in his Pontiac. The second driver out was David Pearson.

Splash 'n' Go Punch

Guaranteed to get your party jumping!

2 cups lemonade
½ cup vodka
1½ ounces crème de menthe
Mint leaves (optional)

Combine the lemonade, vodka and crème de menthe in a pitcher and mix well. Pour over crushed ice in glasses. Serve with a straw. Garnish with mint leaves.

Omit the vodka and substitute crème de menthe syrup for the liqueur for a nonalcoholic beverage.

Yield: *2 servings*

Hot Mulled Cranberry Punch

1 quart water
1 cup sugar
12 whole cloves
2 cinnamon sticks, broken
5 tea bags
1 (32-ounce) bottle apple juice
1 (32-ounce) bottle cranberry juice
    cocktail

Combine the water, sugar, cloves and cinnamon sticks in a large saucepan. Bring to a boil. Boil for 5 minutes. Remove from heat. Add the tea bags. Let steep for 5 minutes. Discard the cloves, cinnamon sticks and tea bags.

Stir the apple juice and cranberry juice cocktail into the tea mixture. Bring to a simmer. Simmer until serving time. Ladle into mugs.

Yield: *25 to 30 servings*

Starting
Line

Breakfast, Brunch & Breads

Fresh Fruit Dip

¹/₃ cup sugar
4 teaspoons cornstarch
¹/₄ teaspoon salt
1 cup unsweetened pineapple juice
¹/₄ cup orange juice
2 eggs, beaten
6 ounces cream cheese, softened

Combine the sugar, cornstarch and salt in a saucepan and mix well. Stir in the pineapple juice and orange juice. Cook for 3 to 5 minutes or until thickened, stirring constantly. Add some of the hot mixture to the eggs. Stir the eggs into the hot mixture.

Cook for 3 to 5 minutes over low heat or until slightly thickened, stirring constantly. Cool for 5 minutes. Add the cream cheese. Beat until blended. Spoon into a serving bowl. Chill, covered, until serving time. Serve with assorted bite-size fresh fruit.

Yield: *2 cups*

Nashville star Brenda Lee, who was seventeen at the time, sang the national anthem for the first race at BMS.

Heavenly Dipped Strawberries

These strawberries are very pretty served on a silver platter at a brunch, bridal shower, or luncheon.

20 firm large strawberries with stems
½ cup mascarpone cheese
10 ounces white or semisweet
*   chocolate, finely chopped*
Finely chopped pistachios

Rinse the strawberries and pat dry. Cut a slit in each strawberry from the tip almost to the stem. Pry the tip open approximately ¼ inch. Fill each strawberry with about 1 teaspoon of the mascarpone cheese and smooth the cheese so it is even with the shape of the strawberry.

Place the chocolate in a microwave-safe bowl. Microwave on Medium until the chocolate melts. Let stand for 1 minute; stir. Microwave for 20 to 30 seconds longer if needed for the proper consistency; stir.

Line a baking sheet with foil or waxed paper. Hold each strawberry by the stem end and dip halfway into the melted chocolate. Roll gently in the pistachios. Arrange on the prepared baking sheet. Let stand until set. Dipped berries may be stored, loosely covered, in the refrigerator for up to 12 hours.

You may substitute a mixture of 4 ounces softened cream cheese, 1½ tablespoons whipping cream and 1 tablespoon sour cream for the mascarpone cheese.

Yield: *10 servings*

Easy Cheese Soufflé

Quick, easy, and a lifesaver for today's busy moms.

10 slices buttered bread
8 ounces cheese, shredded
2 cups milk
3 eggs
1 teaspoon salt

Alternate layers of the bread and cheese in a buttered 9×12-inch baking dish until all of the ingredients are used. Whisk the milk, eggs and salt in a bowl until blended. Pour over the prepared layers.

Chill, covered, in the refrigerator for 3 to 10 hours. Bake at 300 degrees for 45 minutes.

Yield: *8 servings*

Cheese Grits

Serve with breakfast or as a tasty side dish for dinner. Grits are a great substitute for macaroni and cheese, adding a different texture to the meal.

6 cups water
1/2 teaspoon salt
1 1/2 cups grits
3 3/4 cups shredded medium-sharp
    Cheddar cheese
1/2 cup (1 stick) butter or margarine
3 eggs, beaten
1 to 2 teaspoons Tabasco sauce or
    hot sauce
1/4 cup shredded medium-sharp
    Cheddar cheese

Bring the water and salt to a boil in a saucepan. Stir in the grits. Cook using package directions. Remove from heat. Stir in 3 3/4 cups cheese and butter. Cook until melted, stirring constantly. Add 1/2 cup of the hot grits to the eggs and mix well. Add the egg mixture to the hot grits mixture and mix well. Stir in the Tabasco sauce.

Spoon the grits mixture into a lightly greased 3-quart baking dish. Bake at 350 degrees for 70 minutes. Sprinkle with 1/4 cup cheese. Bake for 5 minutes longer.

Yield: *8 servings*

Fresh Summer Tomato Tart

A wonderful summer dish to have when tomatoes are at their peak.

1 refrigerator pie pastry
2 cups shredded mozzarella cheese
2 tablespoons chopped fresh basil
3 medium ripe fresh tomatoes,
  peeled, cut into 1/2-inch slices
1 1/2 tablespoons olive oil
1/4 teaspoon salt
1/4 teaspoon pepper
1 tablespoon chopped fresh basil

Fit the pastry into a 10-inch tart pan; trim the edge. Prick the bottom and side of the pastry with a fork. Bake at 400 degrees for 5 minutes. Maintain the oven temperature.

Sprinkle the cheese evenly over the bottom of the baked layer. Top with the 2 tablespoons basil. Arrange the tomatoes over the prepared layers. Brush with the olive oil. Sprinkle with the salt and pepper.

Place the tart pan on a baking sheet on the lower oven rack. Bake for 35 to 40 minutes. Sprinkle with 1 tablespoon basil. Let stand for 5 minutes before serving.

Yield: *8 servings*

Quiche Lorraine

1 tablespoon butter, softened
1 unbaked (10-inch) deep-dish
    pie shell
12 slices crisp-cooked bacon,
    crumbled
1 cup shredded mozzarella cheese
1/3 cup shredded Velveeta cheese
2 cups heavy cream
4 eggs
3/4 teaspoon salt
1/8 teaspoon nutmeg
1/8 teaspoon sugar
1/8 teaspoon cayenne pepper

Spread the butter over the bottom of the pie shell. Sprinkle with the bacon. Top with the mozzarella cheese and Velveeta cheese. Combine the cream and eggs in a mixing bowl. Beat until thickened. Stir in the salt, nutmeg, sugar and cayenne pepper. Pour over the prepared layers.

Bake at 425 degrees for 15 minutes. Reduce the oven temperature to 300 degrees. Bake for 30 minutes longer. Cool slightly before serving. Shredding cheese is easier if the cheese is placed in the freezer for 15 minutes before shredding.

Yield: *6 servings*

Sausage Cheddar Quiche

1 unbaked (10-inch) deep-dish
    pie shell
1 pound bulk hot pork sausage
½ cup chopped onion
¼ cup chopped green bell pepper
2 eggs
1 cup milk
1½ cups shredded Cheddar cheese
1 (4-ounce) can mushrooms, drained
1 teaspoon minced fresh parsley
½ teaspoon basil
⅛ teaspoon granulated garlic
⅛ teaspoon salt
Paprika to taste

Bake the pie shell at 425 degrees for 8 minutes.
Reduce the oven temperature to 350 degrees.
Brown the sausage in a skillet, stirring until
crumbly. Drain the sausage on paper towels,
reserving the pan drippings. Cook the onion
and bell pepper in the reserved pan drippings
until tender, stirring frequently; do not brown.

Whisk the eggs in a bowl until blended. Stir
in the milk. Add the sausage, onion mixture,
cheese, mushrooms, parsley, basil, garlic and salt
and mix well. Pour into the pie shell. Sprinkle
with paprika. Bake at 350 degrees for 50 minutes
or until set. May freeze for future use.

Reduce the fat grams by using reduced-fat
sausage and reduced-fat cheese and substituting
nonfat half-and-half for the milk.

Yield: *8 servings*

The speedway was sold after the 1976 season to Lanny Hester and Gary Baker.

Breakfast Pizza

1 pound pork sausage
6 eggs
1/2 cup milk
1 teaspoon oregano
1 (8-count) can crescent rolls
8 ounces mozzarella cheese,
    shredded
8 ounces sharp Cheddar cheese,
    shredded

Brown the sausage in a skillet, stirring until crumbly; drain. Whisk the eggs, milk and oregano in a bowl until blended.

Spray a 9×13-inch baking pan with nonstick cooking spray. Unroll the crescent roll dough. Separate into rectangles. Pat over the bottom of the pan, pressing edges and perforations to seal. Sprinkle with the sausage. Pour the egg mixture over the top. Sprinkle with the mozzarella cheese and Cheddar cheese. Bake at 350 degrees for 30 to 35 minutes or until light brown.

Yield: *6 servings*

Spicy Sausage Squares

1 cup baking mix
1/3 cup milk
2 tablespoons mayonnaise
1 pound hot sausage
1/2 cup chopped onion
1 egg
2 tablespoons mayonnaise
2 cups shredded sharp Cheddar
    cheese
2 (4-ounce) cans green chiles,
    drained, chopped

Combine the baking mix, milk and 2 tablespoons mayonnaise in a bowl and mix well. Pat over the bottom of a greased 9×12-inch baking dish.

Brown the sausage with the onion in a skillet, stirring until the sausage is crumbly; drain. Spread the sausage mixture in the prepared dish. Whisk the egg in a bowl until blended. Stir in 2 tablespoons mayonnaise. Add the cheese and green chiles and mix well. Spread the green chile mixture over the top.

Bake at 375 degrees for 25 minutes. Cool slightly. Cut into squares.

Yield: *12 servings*

Southern Spoon Bread

2 cups milk
1 cup cornmeal
1 cup milk
2 tablespoons melted shortening or
    vegetable oil
1 teaspoon salt
1 teaspoon baking powder
3 egg yolks, beaten
3 egg whites, stiffly beaten

Combine 2 cups milk and cornmeal in a saucepan and mix well. Cook over medium heat until of the consistency of mush, stirring frequently; do not boil. Remove from heat. Stir in 1 cup milk, shortening, salt and baking powder. Add the egg yolks and mix well. Fold in the egg whites.

Spoon the cornmeal mixture into a greased 2-quart baking dish. Bake at 325 degrees for 1 hour. Serve immediately, topped with butter.

Yield: *8 servings*

In the spring of 1978, the track name was changed to Bristol International Raceway.

Blueberry Poppy Seed Coffee Cake

Blueberry Filling

¹/₃ cup sugar
2 teaspoons flour
¹/₄ teaspoon nutmeg
2 cups fresh or drained frozen
  blueberries

For the filling, combine the sugar, flour and nutmeg in a bowl and mix well. Add the blueberries and toss gently to coat.

Coffee Cake

1¹/₂ cups flour
2 tablespoons poppy seeds
¹/₂ teaspoon baking soda
¹/₄ teaspoon salt
²/₃ cup sugar
¹/₂ cup (1 stick) butter or margarine,
  softened
1 egg
2 teaspoons grated lemon zest
¹/₂ cup sour cream

For the coffee cake, combine the flour, poppy seeds, baking soda and salt in a bowl and mix well. Beat the sugar and butter in a mixing bowl until light and fluffy. Add the egg and lemon zest and mix well. Add the flour mixture alternately with the sour cream, beginning and ending with the flour mixture and mixing well after each addition.

Spread the batter over the bottom and 1 inch up the side of a greased and floured 9- or 10-inch springform pan. Spreading the batter is made easier by using a rubber spatula sprayed with nonstick cooking spray. Sprinkle with the filling.

Bake at 350 degrees for 45 to 50 minutes or until golden brown. Cool slightly. Remove the side of the pan. Place the coffee cake on a serving platter.

Glaze

¹/₃ cup confectioners' sugar
1 to 2 teaspoons milk

For the glaze, combine the confectioners' sugar and milk in a bowl and mix well. Drizzle over the top of the warm coffee cake. Serve warm or at room temperature.

Yield: *12 servings*

Festive Cranberry Coffee Cake

Serve at your next Christmas brunch.

Coffee Cake
2 cups flour
1 teaspoon baking soda
1/2 teaspoon salt
1 cup sugar
1/2 cup (1 stick) margarine, softened
1 cup sour cream
2 eggs
1/2 cup chopped pecans
1 teaspoon vanilla extract
1 (16-ounce) can whole cranberry
    sauce

For the coffee cake, sift the flour, baking soda and salt into a bowl and mix well. Beat the sugar and margarine in a mixing bowl until light and fluffy. Add the sour cream and eggs and beat until smooth. Add the dry ingredients and beat until blended. Stir in the pecans and vanilla.

Spread half the batter in a greased bundt pan. Spread with the cranberry sauce. Top with the remaining batter. Bake at 350 degrees for 55 to 60 minutes or until the coffee cake tests done. Cool in the pan for 5 to 10 minutes. Invert onto a serving platter.

Glaze
3/4 cup confectioners' sugar
1 tablespoon water
1/2 teaspoon almond extract

For the glaze, combine the confectioners' sugar, water and flavoring in a bowl and mix well. Drizzle over the warm coffee cake.

Yield: *16 servings*

Butterscotch Sticky Buns

2½ tablespoons butter
2 (8-count) cans crescent rolls
2 cups (12 ounces) butterscotch chips
2½ tablespoons butter
½ cup chopped pecans
¼ cup sugar
1½ teaspoons lemon juice
1½ teaspoons water
1 teaspoon cinnamon

Heat 2½ tablespoons butter in a 9×13-inch baking pan until melted; tilt the pan to ensure even coverage.

Unroll the crescent roll dough. Separate into triangles. Sprinkle with 1½ cups of the butterscotch chips. Roll to enclose the filling. Arrange seam side down in the prepared pan. Bake at 375 degrees for 15 to 20 minutes or until brown.

Combine the remaining ½ cup butterscotch chips, 2½ tablespoons butter, pecans, sugar, lemon juice, water and cinnamon in a saucepan. Cook until the butterscotch chips melt, stirring frequently. Pour over the rolls. Bake for 5 minutes longer or until bubbly. Remove to a serving platter immediately.

Yield: *16 servings*

In August of 1978, the first night race was held on the oval.

Cream Cheese Braids

Bread

2 envelopes dry yeast
$^1\!/_2$ cup lukewarm water
1 cup sour cream
$^1\!/_2$ cup sugar
$^1\!/_2$ cup (1 stick) margarine, melted
1 teaspoon salt
4 cups flour
2 eggs, beaten
16 ounces cream cheese, softened
$^3\!/_4$ cup sugar
1 egg
2 teaspoons vanilla extract
$^1\!/_8$ teaspoon salt

For the bread, sprinkle the yeast over the lukewarm water in a large bowl and stir until the yeast dissolves. Heat the sour cream in a saucepan over low heat. Remove from heat. Stir in $^1\!/_2$ cup sugar, margarine and 1 teaspoon salt. Let stand until cool. Add the sour cream mixture, flour and 2 eggs to the yeast mixture and mix well. Chill, covered, for 8 to 10 hours. Divide the dough into 4 equal portions. Roll each portion into an 8×12-inch rectangle on a floured surface.

Beat the cream cheese, $^3\!/_4$ cup sugar, 1 egg, vanilla and $^1\!/_8$ teaspoon salt in a mixing bowl until smooth. Spread $^1\!/_4$ of the cream cheese mixture on each rectangle. Roll as for a jelly roll and pinch the edge to seal. Fold the ends slightly under. Arrange the rolls seam side down on 2 greased baking sheets. Make slits $^2\!/_3$ through the tops of the rolls at 2-inch intervals. Let rise, covered, until doubled in bulk. Bake at 375 degrees for 12 to 15 minutes.

Glaze

2 cups confectioners' sugar
$^1\!/_4$ cup milk
2 teaspoons vanilla extract

For the glaze, combine the confectioners' sugar, milk and vanilla in a bowl and mix well. Drizzle over the warm braids.

Yield: *4 braids*

Overnight Company French Toast

A quick and easy breakfast for the morning before the race.

¼ cup (½ stick) butter or margarine,
    melted
12 (¾-inch) slices French bread
6 eggs
½ cup milk
¼ cup sugar
2 tablespoons maple syrup
1 teaspoon vanilla extract
¼ teaspoon cinnamon
½ teaspoon salt
Confectioners' sugar (optional)
Maple syrup

Coat the bottom of a baking sheet with sides with the butter. Arrange the bread in a single layer over the butter. Whisk the eggs, milk, sugar, 2 tablespoons maple syrup, vanilla, cinnamon and salt in a bowl until blended. Pour half the egg mixture over the bread; turn the bread. Pour the remaining egg mixture over the bread. Chill, covered with plastic wrap, for 8 to 10 hours.

Bake at 400 degrees for 10 minutes; turn the bread. Bake for 5 minutes longer or until brown. Sprinkle each serving with confectioners' sugar and drizzle with maple syrup.

Yield: *6 servings*

Peaches and Cream French Toast

1 (8-ounce) loaf French bread
3 ounces cream cheese, softened
3 tablespoons peach preserves
1 teaspoon brown sugar
½ cup milk
3 eggs
½ teaspoon vanilla extract
¼ teaspoon cinnamon
Confectioners' sugar
Maple syrup

Cut the loaf into eight 1-inch slices. Make a horizontal slit to but not through the bottom edge of each slice to form a pocket.

Combine the cream cheese, preserves and brown sugar in a bowl and mix well. Spoon about 1 tablespoon of the cream cheese mixture into each pocket. Whisk the milk, eggs, vanilla and cinnamon in a bowl until blended. Dip the bread slices into the egg mixture, allowing the excess to drip off.

Spray a skillet or griddle with nonstick cooking spray. Arrange the bread slices in batches in the skillet. Cook over medium heat for 2 minutes per side or until golden brown, turning once. Sprinkle each serving lightly with confectioners' sugar. Serve with maple syrup.

Yield: *4 servings*

On May 28, 1996, the track's name was officially changed to Bristol Motor Speedway.

French Breakfast Puffs

1½ cups flour
1½ teaspoons baking powder
½ teaspoon salt
¼ teaspoon nutmeg
⅛ teaspoon cinnamon
½ cup sugar
⅓ cup shortening
1 egg
½ cup milk
½ cup (1 stick) butter, melted
Cinnamon and sugar

Combine the flour, baking powder, salt, nutmeg and ⅛ teaspoon cinnamon in a bowl and mix well. Combine ½ cup sugar, shortening and egg in a mixing bowl. Beat until smooth. Add the flour mixture and milk. Beat until creamy, scraping the bowl occasionally.

Fill greased miniature muffin cups ¾ full. Bake at 350 degrees for 10 to 15 minutes or until golden brown. Cool in pans for several minutes. Remove to a wire rack to cool completely. Dip the muffins in the melted butter and roll in cinnamon and sugar.

May bake in regular muffins cups. Increase the baking time to 20 minutes.

Yield: *3 dozen puffs*

Low-Fat Blueberry Muffins

¼ cup egg substitute, or 1 egg
1 cup plain yogurt
3 tablespoons margarine, melted
2½ cups baking mix
½ cup sugar
1 cup fresh or frozen blueberries

Beat the egg substitute lightly in a bowl. Fold in the yogurt and margarine. Stir in the baking mix and sugar. Fold in the blueberries.

Fill 12 greased or paper-lined muffin cups ⅔ full. Bake at 400 degrees for 15 minutes or until the muffins test done.

Yield: *1 dozen muffins*

Refrigerator Bran Muffins

3 cups All-Bran
1 cup boiling water
2½ cups flour
2½ teaspoons baking soda
¼ teaspoon salt
2 cups buttermilk
1¼ cups sugar
½ cup shortening
2 eggs, lightly beaten
½ cup chopped nuts
½ cup raisins (optional)
½ cup chopped dates (optional)

Combine the cereal and boiling water in a bowl and mix well. Let stand for 5 minutes; stir. Sift the flour, baking soda and salt into a bowl and mix well.

Add the buttermilk, sugar, shortening and eggs to the cereal mixture and mix well. Add the flour mixture, stirring just until moistened. Fold in the nuts, raisins and dates.

Fill greased muffin cups ¾ full. Bake at 375 degrees for 20 to 25 minutes or until the muffins test done. Remove to a wire rack to cool. May store the muffin batter in the refrigerator.

Yield: *1½ to 2 dozen muffins*

Sour Cream Banana Bread

Children love to eat this bread as well as to help prepare it.

1½ cups sugar
1 cup mashed ripe bananas
    (about 3 bananas)
¾ cup (1½ sticks) butter, softened
2 eggs
¼ cup sour cream
2 cups flour
1 teaspoon baking soda
¼ teaspoon salt
1 teaspoon vanilla extract

Combine the sugar, bananas, butter, eggs and sour cream in a mixing bowl and mix well. Add a mixture of the flour, baking soda and salt. Stir in the vanilla. Beat for 1 to 2 minutes or until blended, scraping the bowl occasionally.

Spoon the batter into a 5×9-inch loaf pan sprayed with nonstick baking spray. Bake at 350 degrees for 30 to 45 minutes or until the loaf tests done. Cool in pan for 10 minutes. Remove the loaf to a wire rack and wrap the warm loaf tightly in plastic wrap to preserve moistness.

Yield: *1 loaf*

Sweet Potato Pecan Bread

1½ cups flour
2 teaspoons baking powder
1 teaspoon nutmeg
½ teaspoon cinnamon
¼ teaspoon salt
1 cup sugar
½ cup vegetable oil
2 eggs, lightly beaten
2 tablespoons milk
1 cup mashed cooked sweet potatoes
    or canned sweet potatoes
1½ cups chopped pecans

Grease the bottom of a 5×9-inch loaf pan. Combine the flour, baking power, nutmeg, cinnamon and salt in a bowl and mix well. Stir in the sugar, oil, eggs and milk. Add the sweet potatoes and pecans and mix well.

Spoon the batter into the prepared loaf pan. Bake at 325 degrees for 70 minutes or until a wooden pick inserted in the center comes out clean. Cool in pan for 10 minutes. Remove to a wire rack to cool completely. May substitute canned pumpkin for the sweet potatoes.

Yield: *1 loaf*

Irish Bread

¼ cup (½ stick) butter, softened
4 cups flour
1 teaspoon baking soda
1 teaspoon salt
½ teaspoon baking powder
2 cups raisins
1 cup chopped walnuts (optional)
2 tablespoons caraway seeds
    (optional)
2 cups milk or buttermilk
¼ cup confectioners' sugar
2 to 3 tablespoons water or milk

Place the butter in a large bowl. Sift the flour, baking soda, salt and baking powder over the butter. Cut in the flour mixture until crumbly. Stir in the raisins, walnuts and caraway seeds. Add the milk and mix until an easily handled dough forms.

Shape the dough into a loaf and place in a greased 5×9-inch loaf pan. Make a horizontal slit and a vertical slit in the shape of a cross in the top of the loaf. Bake at 375 degrees for 70 minutes. Cool in pan for 10 minutes. Remove to a wire rack to cool completely.

Combine the confectioners' sugar and water in a bowl and mix well. Drizzle over the cooled loaf. May bake in 2 miniature loaf pans, decreasing the oven temperature to 350 degrees and the time to 45 minutes.

Yield: *1 loaf*

On April 1, 1982, Lanny Hester sold his half of the speedway to Warner Hodgdon.

Potato Refrigerator Rolls

1 cup unseasoned mashed cooked
    potatoes
²⁄₃ cup shortening
½ cup sugar
1 teaspoon salt
2 eggs, lightly beaten
1 envelope dry yeast
½ cup lukewarm potato cooking
    water
1 cup milk, scalded
6 cups flour, sifted
Melted butter

Combine the mashed potatoes, shortening, sugar, salt and eggs in a bowl and mix well. Dissolve the yeast in the lukewarm potato water and mix well. Stir the scalded milk into the yeast mixture. Add the yeast mixture to the potato mixture and mix well. Add the flour and mix until a stiff dough forms.

Knead the dough well on a lightly floured surface. Place the dough in a large bowl and let rise for 1½ to 2 hours or until doubled in bulk. Knead lightly. Brush the surface with melted butter. Place the dough in a large bowl and cover tightly. The dough may be stored in the refrigerator at this point until ready to bake.

Shape the dough as desired into rolls 1½ hours before baking time. Arrange the rolls not quite touching in a baking pan. Let rise, covered, for 45 to 60 minutes. Bake at 400 degrees for 15 to 20 minutes or until light brown.

Yield: *24 to 28 rolls*

Mom's Best Biscuits

2 cups flour
4 teaspoons baking powder
2 teaspoons sugar
1/2 teaspoon salt
1/2 teaspoon cream of tartar
1/4 teaspoon baking soda
1/2 cup shortening
3/4 cup buttermilk

Sift the flour, baking powder, sugar, salt, cream of tartar and baking soda into a bowl and mix well. Cut in the shortening until crumbly. Add the buttermilk and mix until an easily handled dough forms.

Knead the dough 8 to 10 times on a lightly floured surface. Roll the dough 3/4 inch thick on floured waxed paper. Cut with a biscuit cutter.

Arrange the biscuits on a shiny baking sheet sprayed with nonstick cooking spray. Bake at 450 degrees for 8 to 10 minutes or until golden brown.

Yield: *8 biscuits*

Fiesta Corn Bread

1 cup cornmeal
1/2 teaspoon salt
1/2 teaspoon baking soda
1 cup cream-style corn
2/3 cup buttermilk
1/2 cup shortening, melted
1 (4-ounce) can diced green chiles
2 eggs, lightly beaten
1 cup shredded sharp Cheddar
    cheese

Combine the cornmeal, salt and baking soda in a bowl and mix well. Stir in the corn, buttermilk, shortening, green chiles and eggs. Pour half the batter into a hot greased 9-inch baking pan. Sprinkle with the cheese. Spread with the remaining batter. Bake at 375 degrees for 30 to 40 minutes or until golden brown and crisp.

Yield: *6 to 9 servings*

Pit Crew

Soups, Sandwiches & Snacks

Chilled Cantaloupe and Champagne Soup

The Peppermill Restaurant located in Abingdon, Virginia, contributed this recipe.

1 ripe cantaloupe, chopped
2 cups Champagne
¼ cup sugar

Process the cantaloupe in a blender or food processor until puréed. Add the Champagne and sugar. Process until blended. Chill, covered, for 1 hour. Ladle into soup bowls. May store, covered, in the refrigerator for up to 2 days.

Yield: *4 servings*

Chilled Cream of Zucchini Soup

Abingdon General Store located in Abingdon, Virginia, contributed this recipe.

½ cup (1 stick) butter
4 pounds zucchini, chopped
½ cup chopped onion
½ cup water
2 quarts chicken stock
2 cups heavy cream
2 tablespoons curry powder
Salt and pepper to taste
1 cup sour cream
Fresh herbs

Heat the butter in a saucepan until melted. Stir in the zucchini, onion and water. Simmer for 10 minutes, stirring occasionally; do not brown. Stir in the stock, cream, curry powder, salt and pepper. Remove from heat. Let stand until cool.

Process the soup in batches in a food processor or blender until smooth. Chill, covered, for 8 to 10 hours. Ladle into soup bowls. Top each serving with a dollop of sour cream. Sprinkle with fresh herbs.

Yield: *16 servings*

Country Bean Soup

1¼ cups dried cannellini
6 cups water
2 tablespoons butter
1 tablespoon vegetable oil
1 yellow onion, chopped
1 cup chopped carrots
¼ cup chopped fresh parsley
2 ribs celery with leaves, chopped
2 garlic cloves, minced
4 cups chicken broth
2 cups chopped cabbage (optional)
1 cup elbow macaroni
1 bay leaf
½ teaspoon thyme, crushed
Salt and cracked pepper to taste

Sort and rinse the beans. Combine the beans with a generous amount of water in a 4-quart Dutch oven. Let stand for 8 to 10 hours; drain. Stir in 6 cups water. Bring to a boil; reduce heat. Simmer, covered, for 1 hour or until the beans are tender, stirring occasionally. Drain the beans and transfer to a bowl.

Heat the butter and oil in the Dutch oven until the butter melts. Add the onion, carrots, parsley, celery and garlic and mix well. Cook for 5 minutes, stirring occasionally. Stir in the beans, broth, cabbage, macaroni, bay leaf and thyme.

Simmer for 12 to 15 minutes or until the pasta is tender, stirring occasionally. Discard the bay leaf. Season with salt and pepper. Ladle into soup bowls.

Yield: *6 servings*

In twenty-one of thirty-eight years since Bristol opened, a driver who won a Winston Cup race at Bristol went on to win the series title later the same year.

Baked Potato Soup

4 large baking potatoes
2/3 cup butter or margarine
2/3 cup flour
6 cups milk
12 slices crisp-cooked bacon,
　　crumbled
1 cup shredded Cheddar cheese
4 green onions, chopped
3/4 teaspoon salt
1/2 teaspoon pepper
1 cup sour cream
1/4 cup shredded Cheddar cheese

Prick the potatoes several times with a fork. Bake at 400 degrees for 1 hour or until tender. Let stand until cool. Cut the potatoes lengthwise into halves and scoop the pulp into a bowl. Discard the potato shells.

Heat the butter in a saucepan over low heat until melted. Add the flour and mix until blended. Cook for 1 minute, stirring constantly. Add the milk gradually, stirring constantly. Cook over medium heat until thickened, stirring constantly. Add the potato pulp, 1/2 cup of the bacon, 1 cup cheese, 2 tablespoons of the green onions, salt and pepper.

Cook until heated through, stirring frequently. Stir in the sour cream. May add additional milk at this time for a thinner consistency. Ladle into soup bowls. Serve with the remaining bacon, remaining green onions and 1/4 cup cheese.

Yield: *10 to 12 servings*

Cream of Pumpkin Soup

Great at Thanksgiving.

1 large onion, sliced
¼ cup (½ stick) butter
½ teaspoon curry powder
2 cups canned pumpkin
1½ teaspoons salt
2 cups heavy cream
2½ cups chicken broth
5 teaspoons sour cream
Chopped fresh parsley
Cinnamon to taste

Sauté the onion in the butter in a saucepan until tender. Sprinkle with the curry powder. Sauté for 1 to 2 minutes longer. Remove from heat.

Process the onion mixture, pumpkin and salt in a food processor for 10 seconds, adding the heavy cream while processing. Remove the pumpkin mixture to a large saucepan. Stir in the broth.

Cook over low heat until heated through, stirring frequently. Ladle into soup bowls. Top each serving with 1 teaspoon of the sour cream, chopped parsley and cinnamon.

Yield: *5 servings*

State Street Tomato Bisque

KP Duty in Bristol, Tennessee, contributed this recipe.

¾ to 1 cup shredded carrots
1 rib celery, chopped
½ white onion, chopped
1 (48-ounce) jar marinara sauce
1 to 2 tablespoons butter
1 quart heavy cream
¼ cup packed brown sugar

Process the carrots, celery and onion in a food processor until minced. Press the marinara sauce through a strainer into a bowl until smooth.

Sauté the carrot mixture in the butter in a large saucepan until brown. Stir in the marinara sauce, heavy cream and brown sugar. Simmer until of the desired consistency, stirring frequently. Ladle into soup bowls.

Yield: *8 servings*

Italian Sausage and Tortellini Soup

6 to 8 mild or hot Italian sausage
    links (about 1½ pounds)
3 large carrots, chopped
3 ribs celery, chopped
1 tablespoon olive oil
4 (12-ounce) cans chicken broth or
    6 cups homemade broth
1 (28-ounce) can crushed tomatoes
1 (14-ounce) can quartered artichoke
    hearts, drained, cut into halves
6 scallions, chopped
1 (2-ounce) can sliced black olives,
    drained
¾ teaspoon oregano
¾ teaspoon basil
¾ teaspoon thyme
1 (7-ounce) package tortellini
Salt to taste
Olive oil

Cook the sausage in a skillet until brown and cooked through; drain. Cut into thin slices. Sauté the carrots and celery in 1 tablespoon olive oil in a stockpot. Add the broth, undrained tomatoes, artichokes, scallions, olives, oregano, basil and thyme and mix well.

Simmer for 30 to 45 minutes, stirring occasionally. Cook the pasta using package directions in boiling salted water in a saucepan until al dente; drain. Toss with a small amount of olive oil in a bowl. Add the pasta to the soup mixture just before serving and mix well. Simmer just until heated through, stirring frequently. Ladle into soup bowls.

Yield: *6 to 8 servings*

Tortilla Soup

4 cups chicken stock
2 boneless skinless chicken breasts
1 (4-ounce) can green chiles, drained,
    chopped
1 medium zucchini, sliced, cut into
    halves or quarters
1 medium onion, chopped
1 (10-ounce) can tomatoes with
    green chiles
2 tablespoons minced fresh cilantro
2 garlic cloves, minced
1 tablespoon lime juice
½ teaspoon cayenne pepper
½ teaspoon cumin
2 (10-inch) flour tortillas
1 to 2 cups vegetable oil
1 cup shredded Monterey Jack cheese
4 slices avocado

Combine the stock and chicken in a large saucepan. Poach the chicken for 25 to 35 minutes or until cooked through. Remove the chicken to a plate with a slotted spoon, reserving the broth in the pan. Chop the chicken into bite-size pieces.

Return the chicken to the stock. Stir in the green chiles, zucchini, onion, undrained tomatoes, cilantro, garlic, lime juice, cayenne pepper and cumin. Bring to a boil; reduce heat. Simmer until the vegetables are tender, stirring occasionally.

Cut the tortillas into ¼-inch strips. Cut the strips into 2- to 3-inch strips. Add enough of the oil to a skillet to measure ½ inch. Fry the tortilla strips in the hot oil until golden brown; drain.

Ladle the soup into soup bowls. Top with the tortilla strips, cheese and sliced avocado.

Yield: *4 servings*

Shrimp Bisque

1 pound deveined peeled cooked
    shrimp
¼ cup (½ stick) butter, softened
3 tablespoons (heaping) flour
1 quart milk
½ cup heavy cream
1 tablespoon lemon juice
¾ tablespoon A-1 steak sauce or
    Worcestershire sauce
½ teaspoon salt, or to taste
¼ teaspoon white pepper, or to taste
⅛ teaspoon hot sauce
6 tablespoons sherry (optional)
1 lemon, thinly sliced (optional)

Process the shrimp in a blender until ground. Combine the butter and flour in a large saucepan and mix until of a paste consistency. Add the milk gradually, stirring constantly. Add the cream gradually, stirring constantly. Cook over medium heat until thickened, stirring constantly. Stir in the shrimp, lemon juice, A.1. steak sauce, salt, white pepper and hot sauce. Cook just until heated through, stirring occasionally; do not boil.

Ladle into soup bowls. Add 1 tablespoon sherry to each serving if desired. Top with a lemon slice.

Yield: *6 servings*

In the fall of 1969, BMS was reshaped and remeasured. The turns were banked at 36 degrees and it became a .5333-mile oval.

Spicy White Bean Chili

2 medium white onions, chopped
1 garlic clove, minced, or ⅛ teaspoon
    garlic powder
1 tablespoon vegetable oil
5 medium boneless skinless chicken
    breasts, cooked, chopped
    (about 4 cups)
3 (16-ounce) cans Great Northern
    beans, drained
5 cups chicken broth
2 (4-ounce) cans chopped green
    chiles, drained
2 tablespoons cumin
1½ teaspoons chili powder
¼ teaspoon cayenne pepper
¼ teaspoon oregano
¼ teaspoon ground cloves
⅛ teaspoon paprika
2 cups shredded Monterey Jack
    cheese

Sauté the onions and garlic in the oil in a stockpot until the onions are tender. Add the chicken, beans, broth, green chiles, cumin, chili powder, cayenne pepper, oregano, cloves and paprika and mix well. Bring to a boil; reduce heat.

Simmer for 1 hour, stirring occasionally. Ladle into soup bowls. Sprinkle with the cheese.

Yield: *8 to 10 servings*

Creole Gumbo

Great wintertime soup.

4 chicken breasts, skinned
6 cups water
2 (28-ounce) cans diced tomatoes
2 (14-ounce) cans French-style green beans, drained
2 (10-ounce) packages frozen lima beans
4 teaspoons Creole seasoning
2 teaspoons chili powder
2 teaspoons paprika
2 bay leaves
1/2 teaspoon garlic powder
1/2 teaspoon onion powder
1/4 teaspoon red pepper
1/8 teaspoon hot sauce
1/8 teaspoon soy sauce
2 (15-ounce) cans black beans, drained, rinsed

Combine the chicken, water, undrained tomatoes, green beans, lima beans, Creole seasoning, chili powder, paprika, bay leaves, garlic powder, onion powder, red pepper, hot sauce and soy sauce in a Dutch oven and mix well; cover. Bring to a boil over medium heat; reduce heat.

Simmer for 1 hour, stirring occasionally. Remove the chicken with a slotted spoon to a plate. Chop the chicken into bite-size pieces, discarding the bone. Return the chicken to the soup. Add the black beans and mix well. Cook just until heated through, stirring occasionally. Discard the bay leaves. Ladle into soup bowls. May freeze for future use.

Yield: *16 to 20 servings*

Souped-Up Red Beans and Rice

1 pound dried red beans
1 pound smoked link sausage,
    cut into 1-inch slices
1 ham hock
3 medium onions, chopped
1 bunch green onions, chopped
3 ribs celery, chopped
3 garlic cloves, minced
2 bay leaves
1 tablespoon Worcestershire sauce
1 tablespoon salt
1 teaspoon black pepper
½ teaspoon red pepper
½ teaspoon oregano
½ teaspoon thyme
3 dashes of Tabasco sauce
Hot cooked rice

Rinse and sort the beans. Combine the beans with enough water to cover in a bowl. Let stand for 8 to 10 hours; drain.

Combine the beans with enough water to cover in a Dutch oven. Stir in the sausage, ham hock, onions, green onions, celery, garlic, bay leaves, Worcestershire sauce, salt, black pepper, red pepper, oregano, thyme and Tabasco sauce. Bring to a boil; reduce heat.

Simmer for 1 hour or until the beans are tender, stirring occasionally. Discard the bay leaves. Ladle over hot cooked rice in soup bowls. Serve with crusty French bread.

The flavor of the soup is enhanced if prepared 1 day in advance and stored, covered, in the refrigerator. Skim the fat from the soup and reheat before serving. This recipe is very spicy and may require adjusting of spices for those less adventurous.

Yield: *8 servings*

Grilled Portobello Mushroom Sandwich

Chef Karl P. Harris of The Brooklyn Grill, located in Bristol, Virginia, contributed this recipe.

1 tablespoon olive oil
1 garlic clove, crushed
½ teaspoon chopped fresh basil
1 (6-ounce) portobello cap
2 ounces Swiss cheese
1 kaiser roll, split
1½ teaspoons mayonnaise
1 slice red onion
2 slices fresh tomato
4 to 6 leaves wild greens
Salt and pepper to taste

Combine the olive oil, garlic and basil in a bowl and mix well. Brush both sides of the portobello cap with the olive oil mixture. Arrange on a grill rack on a preheated grill. Grill for 3 to 4 minutes per side, turning once. Place the Swiss cheese on the portobello cap. Grill until the cheese melts. Remove from heat.

Grill both cut sides of the roll. Spread the mayonnaise on both grilled sides of the rolls. Arrange the portobello cap on 1 roll half. Top with the onion, tomato slices and wild greens. Sprinkle with salt and pepper. Top with the remaining roll half. Serve with vegetable chips.

Yield: *1 sandwich*

The Bristol Chamber estimates the economic impact of the August 2000 race at $503,928,000 indirect and $111,984,600 direct for the Tri-Cities area.

Picnic Sandwiches for a Crowd

3 ounces cream cheese, softened
²/₃ cup mayonnaise
2 tablespoons chopped green onions
2 (1-pound) loaves French bread
8 slices cooked ham
8 slices roasted turkey
8 slices salami
8 slices summer salami
4 cups torn lettuce
¼ cup Italian salad dressing
2 medium tomatoes, sliced

Combine the cream cheese, mayonnaise and green onions in a bowl and mix well. Cut the bread loaves horizontally into halves.

Spread the cream cheese mixture on the bottom half of each loaf. Fold the ham, turkey, salami and summer salami slices into halves. Arrange 4 folded slices of each over the cream cheese mixture on each bread bottom. Toss the lettuce and salad dressing in a bowl until coated. Spoon the lettuce mixture over the prepared layers. Top with the tomatoes. Cover with the bread tops. Cut each loaf into quarters.

May also add your favorite cheese or cheeses, sliced olives and/or hot peppers to the sandwiches.

Yield: *8 servings*

Fresh-Baked Reuben Loaf

3¼ cups (about) flour
1 tablespoon sugar
1 teaspoon salt
1 envelope fast-rising yeast
1 cup hot (125 to 130 degrees) water
1 tablespoon butter, softened
¼ cup Thousand Island salad
    dressing
6 ounces corned beef, thinly sliced
4 ounces Swiss cheese, thinly sliced
1 (8-ounce) can shredded sauerkraut,
    drained
1 egg white, beaten
2 teaspoons caraway seeds (optional)

Combine 2¼ cups of the flour, sugar, salt and yeast in a bowl and mix well. Stir in the hot water and butter. Add just enough of the remaining 1 cup flour to make a soft dough and mix well. Knead the dough on a lightly floured surface for 4 minutes.

Roll the dough into a 10×14-inch rectangle on a greased baking sheet. Spread the salad dressing horizontally in the center of the rectangle. Top with the corned beef, Swiss cheese and sauerkraut in the order listed.

Cut 1-inch strips from the outer edge of the rectangle to the filling on both sides. Fold the strips alternately across the filling. Brush with the egg white. Sprinkle with the caraway seeds.

Place the baking sheet over a shallow pan of boiling water. Let the dough rise for 15 minutes. Bake at 400 degrees for 25 minutes or until golden brown. Cool slightly. Cut into 1-inch slices.

Yield: *10 servings*

Supreme Ham Sandwiches

Pack these sandwiches in a cooler and warm over hot coals on race day.

Mustard Poppy Seed Sauce
1 cup (2 sticks) butter or margarine,
    softened
1 medium onion, finely chopped
3 tablespoons prepared mustard
1½ teaspoons poppy seeds (optional)
1 teaspoon Worcestershire sauce

For the sauce, combine the butter, onion, prepared mustard, poppy seeds and Worcestershire sauce in a bowl and mix well.

Sandwiches
8 large hamburger buns, split
12 ounces shaved or sliced cooked
    ham
8 slices Swiss cheese

For the sandwiches, spread the sauce on the cut sides of the buns. Layer the bun bottoms with the ham and cheese. Top with the bun tops. Wrap each sandwich individually in foil. Heat at 400 degrees for 10 minutes. Serve hot.

May prepare the sandwiches several hours in advance and store in the refrigerator. Heat just before serving.

Yield: *8 sandwiches*

Peanut Butter and Apple Pockets

1 small Granny Smith apple
3 ounces cream cheese, softened
¼ cup creamy peanut butter
2 tablespoons packed brown sugar
⅛ teaspoon cinnamon
1 (24-slice) loaf white or wheat bread

Peel the apple and slice. Chop with a food chopper. Combine the cream cheese, peanut butter, brown sugar and cinnamon in a bowl and mix well. Stir in the apple.

Place 1 tablespoon of the apple filling in the center of each of 12 slices of bread. Top with another bread slice. Cut with a round cookie cutter to seal the sandwiches.

Yield: *12 pockets*

Cracker Candy

40 saltines
1 cup (2 sticks) butter
1 cup packed brown sugar
*2 cups (12 ounces) milk chocolate
   chips*

Arrange the crackers side by side on a foil-lined baking sheet. Combine the butter and brown sugar in a saucepan. Bring to a boil, stirring frequently. Boil for 3 minutes exactly, stirring frequently.

Drizzle the brown sugar mixture over the crackers. Bake at 400 degrees for 4 minutes. Sprinkle with the chocolate chips. Let stand for 5 minutes or until the chocolate chips melt. Spread the chocolate evenly over the crackers. Chill until set. Break into pieces. Store in the refrigerator. Do not substitute margarine for the butter in this recipe.

Yield: *20 servings*

Praline Crunch

Beware; this is an addictive snack.

8 cups Quaker Oat Squares
2 cups chopped pecans
1/2 cup light corn syrup
1/2 cup packed brown sugar
1/4 cup (1/2 stick) butter or margarine
1 teaspoon vanilla extract
1/2 teaspoon baking soda
1 (12- to 16-ounce) package dried
    cranberries

Combine the cereal and pecans in a 9×13-inch baking pan. Combine the corn syrup, brown sugar and butter in a saucepan. Cook until the butter melts, stirring constantly. Bring to a boil. Remove from heat. Stir in the vanilla and baking soda.

Pour the syrup mixture over the cereal mixture and stir until the cereal mixture is evenly coated. Bake at 250 degrees for 1 hour, stirring every 20 minutes. Spread on a baking sheet to cool. Break into pieces. Combine the cereal mixture with the cranberries in a bowl and mix well. Store in an airtight container.

Yield: *10 cups*

Sugared Pecans

1 egg white
1 tablespoon water
1 pound pecan halves
1 cup sugar
1 teaspoon (heaping) salt
1 teaspoon cinnamon

Whisk the egg white and water in a bowl until foamy. Add the pecans and stir until the pecans are coated and the mixture has been absorbed.

Combine the sugar, salt and cinnamon in a sealable plastic bag. Add the pecans. Seal tightly and shake to coat. Spread the pecans on an insulated baking sheet. Bake at 275 degrees for 45 minutes, stirring every 15 minutes. Let stand until cool. Store in an airtight container.

Yield: *8 to 12 servings*

Green
Flag

Salads

Bleu Cheese Walnut Salad

Dijon Vinaigrette
$^1\!/_3$ cup red wine vinegar
$^1\!/_4$ cup Dijon mustard
$^3\!/_4$ cup vegetable oil
$^1\!/_4$ cup sour cream

For the vinaigrette, whisk the wine vinegar and Dijon mustard in a bowl until blended. Whisk in the oil and sour cream.

Salad
2 (10-ounce) packages European
    mixed salad greens
1 cup walnuts, toasted, chopped
1 medium red onion, thinly sliced
4 ounces bleu cheese, crumbled

For the salad, toss the salad greens, walnuts, onion and bleu cheese in a salad bowl. Add the vinaigrette and toss to coat. Serve immediately.

Yield: *8 to 10 servings*

Parrish's Salad

Red Wine Vinaigrette
$^3\!/_4$ cup vegetable oil
$^3\!/_4$ cup sugar
$^3\!/_4$ cup red wine vinegar
3 garlic cloves, minced
$^1\!/_2$ teaspoon salt
$^1\!/_2$ teaspoon pepper

For the vinaigrette, combine the oil, sugar, wine vinegar, garlic, salt and pepper in a jar with a tight-fitting lid. Seal and shake to mix.

Salad
1 head romaine, torn into
    bite-size pieces
8 ounces Monterey Jack cheese,
    shredded
1 cup walnut or pecans halves,
    toasted
1 quart strawberries, cut into quarters

For the salad, toss the romaine, cheese, walnuts and strawberries in a bowl. Add the vinaigrette just before serving and toss to coat.

Yield: *8 to 10 servings*

Spinach Salad with Poppy Seed Dressing

Poppy Seed Dressing
3/4 cup canola oil
1/4 cup cider vinegar
1/4 cup finely chopped fresh or
*   dehydrated onion*
1/4 cup sugar
2 tablespoons poppy seeds
3/4 teaspoon salt
3/4 teaspoon dry mustard

Salad
1 bunch spinach, trimmed, torn
8 slices crisp-cooked bacon, crumbled
1 (11-ounce) can mandarin oranges,
*   drained*
1 avocado, chopped
5 thin slices purple or yellow onion,
*   separated into rings*
1 cup croutons

For the dressing, combine the canola oil, vinegar, onion, sugar, poppy seeds, salt and dry mustard in a jar with a tight-fitting lid. Seal tightly and shake to mix. May process the dressing in a blender or food processor.

For the salad, toss the spinach, bacon, mandarin oranges, avocado and onion in a bowl. Add the croutons and about 1/2 cup or the desired amount of the dressing and toss to coat. Serve immediately.

Yield: *6 servings*

Granny Smith Spinach Salad

Cider Vinaigrette
1/4 cup sugar
1/4 cup olive oil
2 tablespoons apple cider vinegar
1/4 teaspoon celery salt
1/8 teaspoon white pepper

For the dressing, process the sugar, olive oil, vinegar, celery salt and white pepper in a food processor until blended.

Salad
12 ounces baby spinach
2 Granny Smith apples, chopped
1/2 cup salted cashews
1/4 cup raisins

For the salad, toss the spinach, apples, cashews and raisins in a bowl. Add the dressing and toss to coat. Great with seafood entrées and roasted turkey.

Yield: *4 to 6 servings*

Tullamore Greens

Orange Dressing
1/4 cup vegetable oil
2 tablespoons thawed frozen orange
   juice concentrate
1 tablespoon honey
1/4 teaspoon salt
1/8 teaspoon freshly ground pepper

For the dressing, combine the oil, orange juice concentrate, honey, salt and pepper in a jar with a tight-fitting lid. Seal tightly and shake to mix.

Salad
4 heads Bibb lettuce, separated into
   leaves
1 cup cubed Swiss cheese
1 firm ripe peach, sliced
1 (8-ounce) can pineapple tidbits,
   drained
1/2 cup purple grape halves, seeded
1/4 cup walnut halves

For the salad, toss the lettuce, cheese, peach, pineapple, grapes and walnuts in a bowl. Drizzle with the dressing and toss to coat.

Yield: *4 to 6 servings*

Winter Solstice Salad with Cranberry Port Vinaigrette

Cranberry Port Vinaigrette
1 cup tawny port
½ cup packed thinly sliced shallots
1 cup fresh cranberries
⅓ cup canola oil
3 tablespoons raspberry vinegar
Salt and pepper to taste

For the vinaigrette, combine the wine and shallots in a small heavy saucepan. Bring to a boil. Boil for 10 minutes or until the liquid is reduced to 2 tablespoons, stirring occasionally. Stir in the cranberries, canola oil and raspberry vinegar. Bring to a boil. Boil for 3 minutes, stirring occasionally. Season with salt and pepper. Remove from heat. Cool slightly.

Salad
8 cups torn romaine
⅔ cup crumbled Stilton cheese
¼ cup chopped pistachios

For the salad, place the romaine in a large salad bowl. Drizzle with the warm vinaigrette and toss to coat. Sprinkle with the cheese and pistachios and toss lightly. Serve warm with crusty bread.

Yield: *6 servings*

One race at the BMS results in an average of 60,000 cars parked, more than 200 tons of garbage, and more than 27,000 hot dogs sold.

High Bank Overnight Salad

1 head lettuce, chopped
1 to 1½ cups frozen peas, thawed
½ cup chopped celery
½ cup chopped green or red
    bell pepper
1 small red onion, chopped
2 cups mayonnaise or reduced-fat
    mayonnaise
¼ cup whole milk or skim milk
2 tablespoons sugar
⅛ teaspoon salt
¾ cup shredded Cheddar cheese
8 to 10 slices crisp-cooked bacon,
    crumbled

Layer the lettuce, peas, celery, bell pepper and onion in the order listed in a deep salad bowl. Combine the mayonnaise, milk, sugar and salt in a bowl and mix well. Spread over the prepared layers. Sprinkle with cheese and top with the bacon.

Chill, covered with foil or plastic wrap, for 8 to 10 hours. Serve layered or toss before serving.

Yield: *10 to 12 servings*

Broccoli Salad Supreme

1 large bunch broccoli
1 red onion, chopped
1 cup cashews (optional)
8 to 10 slices crisp-cooked bacon,
  crumbled
½ cup raisins
1 cup mayonnaise or reduced-fat
  mayonnaise
⅓ to ½ cup sugar
2 to 3 tablespoons vinegar

Discard the tough ends of the broccoli stems. Slice the remaining stems into bite-size pieces. Separate the florets into bite-size portions. Combine the broccoli, onion, cashews, bacon and raisins in a bowl and toss gently.

Combine the mayonnaise, sugar and vinegar in a bowl and mix well. Add to the broccoli mixture and toss to coat. Chill, covered, for 6 to 10 hours.

Yield: *6 to 8 servings*

On July 6, 1983, Warner Hodgdon completed 100 percent purchase of Bristol Motor Speedway, as well as Nashville Motor Speedway, in a buy-sell agreement with Baker. Hodgdon named Larry Carrier as the track's general manager.

Classic Creamy Coleslaw

1 large head cabbage
3 medium carrots, peeled, shredded
1/3 cup finely chopped onion
2 tablespoons sugar
1/2 teaspoon salt
1/2 teaspoon pepper
1/2 cup mayonnaise
3 tablespoons vinegar
1 tablespoon lemon juice
1 teaspoon celery seeds (optional)

Core the cabbage. Cut into 2-inch chunks and thinly slice. Combine the cabbage, carrots and onion in a bowl and mix well. Add the sugar, salt and pepper and toss to mix. Add the mayonnaise, vinegar and lemon juice, tossing after each addition. Stir in the celery seeds. Chill, covered, for 2 to 3 hours before serving.

Yield: *10 to 12 servings*

Piedmont North Carolina-Style Coleslaw

1 medium head cabbage, chilled
2/3 cup ketchup
1/2 cup apple cider vinegar
1/4 cup sugar
1/4 cup packed brown sugar
2 teaspoons salt
2 teaspoons pepper
2 teaspoons hot sauce

Remove the outer leaves of the cabbage. Cut the cabbage into halves and remove the core. Coarsely grate the cabbage into a bowl. Return the cabbage to the refrigerator.

Combine the ketchup, vinegar, sugar, brown sugar, salt, pepper and hot sauce in a bowl and mix well. Add to the chilled cabbage and toss to mix. Let stand for 1 hour before serving.

Yield: *20 servings*

Corn and Black Bean Salad

2 (15-ounce) cans whole kernel corn,
    drained
1 (15-ounce) can black beans,
    drained, rinsed
1 (14-ounce) can hearts of palm,
    drained, sliced
2 large tomatoes, seeded, chopped
1/2 cup chopped purple onion
1/3 cup minced fresh cilantro
1/4 cup vegetable oil
3 tablespoons lime juice
1 1/2 teaspoons chili powder
1/2 teaspoon cumin

Combine the corn, beans, hearts of palm, tomatoes, onion and cilantro in a bowl and mix well. Whisk the oil, lime juice, chili powder and cumin in a bowl. Pour over the corn mixture and toss gently to coat.

Chill, covered, for 3 hours. Spoon the bean mixture onto lettuce-lined salad plates. For variety, serve as an appetizer with tortilla chips.

Yield: *10 to 12 servings*

Shoe Peg Corn Salad

Ginny McClure, wife of Larry McClure

1 (16-ounce) can tiny green peas,
    drained (optional)
1 (15-ounce) can tiny Shoe Peg corn,
    drained
1 (4-ounce) jar chopped pimentos,
    drained
1 bunch green onions, chopped
1 green bell pepper, chopped
1 rib celery, chopped
1 cup vegetable oil
1 cup sugar
1 cup vinegar
1 teaspoon salt
1 teaspoon pepper

Combine the peas, corn, pimentos, green onions, bell pepper and celery in a bowl and mix well. Combine the oil, sugar, vinegar, salt and pepper in a saucepan. Bring to a boil, stirring frequently. Pour the hot oil mixture over the corn mixture and mix well.

Chill, covered, for 8 to 10 hours, stirring occasionally. Drain before serving.

Yield: *12 servings*

Favorite Red Potato Salad

7 unpeeled medium red potatoes,
    chopped
¼ cup chopped green onions
⅓ cup sugar
1 tablespoon cornstarch
1 teaspoon salt
¼ teaspoon dry mustard
½ cup milk
¼ cup white vinegar
¼ cup (½ stick) butter or margarine
1 egg, lightly beaten
¼ cup mayonnaise
½ teaspoon white pepper

Combine the potatoes with enough water to cover in a saucepan. Bring to a boil. Boil until tender; drain. Add the green onions and mix well.

Combine the sugar, cornstarch, salt and dry mustard in a saucepan and mix well. Stir in the milk, vinegar, butter and egg. Cook over medium heat until thickened, stirring constantly. Remove from heat. Stir in the mayonnaise.

Spoon the potato mixture into a bowl. Sprinkle with the white pepper. Add the cooked dressing and toss gently to coat. Chill, covered, in the refrigerator until serving time.

Yield: *6 to 8 servings*

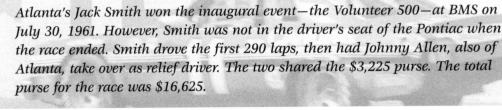

Atlanta's Jack Smith won the inaugural event—the Volunteer 500—at BMS on July 30, 1961. However, Smith was not in the driver's seat of the Pontiac when the race ended. Smith drove the first 290 laps, then had Johnny Allen, also of Atlanta, take over as relief driver. The two shared the $3,225 purse. The total purse for the race was $16,625.

Orzo Artichoke Salad

This salad was served at the 2000 Drivers' Wives Luncheon.

2 tablespoons white wine vinegar
2 tablespoons lemon juice
1 teaspoon Dijon mustard
$^{1}/_{3}$ cup olive oil
$1^{1}/_{2}$ cups orzo
1 (14-ounce) can artichoke hearts,
    drained, chopped
$^{2}/_{3}$ cup grated Parmesan cheese
$^{1}/_{4}$ cup chopped fresh parsley
4 ounces baked Virginia ham, thinly
    sliced, cut into $^{1}/_{2}$-inch pieces
4 green onions, thinly sliced
2 tablespoons chopped fresh basil
Salt and pepper to taste

Combine the wine vinegar, lemon juice and Dijon mustard in a blender or food processor container. Process until mixed. Add the olive oil in a steady stream, processing constantly until blended.

Cook the orzo using package directions; drain. Rinse with cold water and drain. Combine the orzo, artichokes, cheese, parsley, ham, green onions and basil in a bowl and mix gently. Add the olive oil mixture and toss to coat. Season with salt and pepper. Chill, covered, until serving time. Spoon the salad onto a lettuce-lined serving platter.

Yield: *6 servings*

Mediterranean Pasta Salad

8 ounces rotini
1 (6-ounce) jar hearts of palm,
    drained, chopped
1 (4-ounce) can sliced black olives,
    drained
1 cup frozen tiny peas, thawed
1 medium red bell pepper, chopped
½ small purple onion, chopped
½ cup freshly grated Parmesan
    cheese
½ cup mayonnaise
½ cup Italian salad dressing
1 teaspoon parsley flakes
½ teaspoon dillweed
½ teaspoon coarsely ground pepper

Cook the pasta using package directions; drain. Rinse with cold water and drain. Combine the hearts of palm, olives, peas, bell pepper, onion and cheese in a bowl and mix well. Stir in the pasta.

Combine the mayonnaise, salad dressing, parsley flakes, dillweed and pepper in a bowl and mix well. Add to the pasta mixture and mix well. Chill, covered, for 1 hour.

Yield: *8 servings*

Italian Chicken and Pasta Salad

16 ounces linguini
1/2 cup Italian salad dressing
1/2 cup grated Parmesan cheese
3 cups chopped cooked chicken
1 (14-ounce) can artichoke hearts,
  drained, chopped
1 (2-ounce) can chopped black olives,
  drained
1/4 cup chopped fresh parsley
1 green onion, chopped
1 teaspoon oregano
1 teaspoon basil
1 teaspoon garlic salt
1 cup mayonnaise

Cook the pasta using package directions; drain. Rinse with cold water and drain. Toss the pasta, salad dressing and cheese in a bowl. Marinate, covered, in the refrigerator for 8 to 10 hours.

Combine the chicken, artichokes, olives, parsley, green onion, oregano, basil and garlic salt in a bowl and mix well. Stir in the mayonnaise. Chill, covered, for 8 to 10 hours. Combine the chilled pasta mixture and chilled chicken mixture in a bowl and toss to mix.

Yield: *6 to 8 servings*

Grilled Teriyaki Chicken Salad

Cindy Elliott, wife of Bill Elliott

3 boneless skinless chicken breasts
Teriyaki sauce
1 (12-ounce) package fresh broccoli
    coleslaw
1 (12-ounce) package fresh broccoli
    florets
2 bunches green onions, thinly sliced
1 (3-ounce) package ramen beef
    noodles with seasoning packet,
    broken
$\frac{1}{2}$ (5-ounce) can chow mein noodles
$\frac{1}{2}$ cup sliced almonds
1 cup unsalted sunflower seed kernels
$\frac{1}{2}$ cup vegetable oil
$\frac{1}{2}$ cup sugar
$\frac{1}{3}$ cup white vinegar
1 teaspoon sesame oil

Arrange the chicken in a dish. Drizzle with teriyaki sauce, turning to coat. Marinate, covered, in the refrigerator for 1 to 3 hours, turning occasionally. Grill the chicken over hot coals for 5 to 6 minutes per side or until cooked through. Cool slightly. Cut into strips.

Combine the broccoli coleslaw and broccoli florets in a bowl and mix well. Layer the coleslaw mixture, green onions, ramen noodles, chow mein noodles, almonds and sunflower seed kernels $\frac{1}{2}$ at a time in a large salad bowl. Top with the chicken strips.

Whisk the oil, sugar, wine vinegar and sesame oil in a bowl. Add the ramen noodle seasoning from the packet and whisk until blended. Pour the dressing over the prepared layers. Serve immediately.

Yield: *4 to 6 servings*

Tropical Chicken Salad

This salad was served at the 2000 Drivers' Wives Luncheon.

3 boneless skinless chicken breasts
Salt to taste
8 ounces cream cheese, softened
1 (11-ounce) can mandarin oranges,
    drained, chopped
1 (8-ounce) can pineapple tidbits,
    drained
2/3 cup finely chopped celery
1/4 cup chopped pecans
1/2 teaspoon salt
1/2 teaspoon tarragon
1/8 teaspoon white pepper

Cook the chicken in boiling salted water in a saucepan for 20 minutes or until cooked through; drain. Cool slightly and chop the chicken.

Combine the cream cheese, mandarin oranges, pineapple, celery, pecans, salt, tarragon and white pepper in a bowl and mix well. Stir in the chicken. Spoon onto a lettuce-lined serving platter or serve on croissants.

Yield: *6 servings*

In August of 1992, BMS became the first speedway to host a Winston Cup event that boasted an all-concrete track surface.

Shrimp Pasta Salad

Dressing

1/2 cup vegetable oil

1 (4-ounce) jar chopped pimentos,
    drained

1/3 cup cider vinegar

1 teaspoon prepared mustard

1 teaspoon salt

1 garlic clove, minced

Salad

2 cups shell macaroni

12 ounces frozen medium shrimp,
    cooked, drained

1 1/2 cups chopped celery

1/2 cup chopped green bell pepper

For the dressing, whisk the oil, pimentos, vinegar, prepared mustard, salt and garlic in a bowl until mixed.

For the salad, cook the pasta using package directions; drain. Rinse with cold water and drain. Combine the pasta, shrimp, celery and bell pepper in a bowl and mix gently. Add the dressing and toss gently to coat. Chill, covered, for 1 hour or longer before serving. May substitute two 6-ounce cans drained water-pack tuna for the shrimp.

Yield: *12 servings*

Apricot Salad

2 (3-ounce) packages apricot gelatin
$^2/_3$ cup sugar
$^2/_3$ cup water
1 (20-ounce) can crushed pineapple
1 (11-ounce) can mandarin oranges
2 (4-ounce) jars baby food apricots
8 ounces cream cheese, softened
$^1/_2$ cup sweetened condensed milk
$^1/_2$ to 1$^1/_2$ cups finely chopped nuts

Combine the gelatin, sugar and water in a saucepan and mix well. Bring to a boil, stirring constantly. Boil until the sugar and gelatin dissolve, stirring constantly. Remove from heat. Stir in the undrained pineapple, undrained mandarin oranges and apricots. Let stand until cool.

Combine the cream cheese and condensed milk in a mixing bowl. Beat until smooth, scraping the bowl occasionally. Stir in the gelatin mixture. Add the nuts and mix well. Spoon the gelatin mixture into a 9×13-inch dish. Chill, covered, for 8 to 10 hours or until set.

Yield: *12 servings*

A total of forty-two cars started the first race at BMS, but only nineteen finished.

Strawberry Pretzel Salad

2 cups crushed pretzels
¾ cup (1½ sticks) butter, melted
2 tablespoons sugar
8 ounces cream cheese, softened
1 cup sugar
1 cup whipped topping
1 (6-ounce) package strawberry
    gelatin
2 cups boiling water
2 (10-ounce) packages frozen
    sweetened strawberries

Combine the pretzels, butter and 2 tablespoons sugar in a bowl and mix well. Spread over the bottom of a 9×13-inch baking dish. Bake at 400 degrees for 3 minutes. Let stand until cool.

Combine the cream cheese and 1 cup sugar in a mixing bowl. Beat until blended. Fold in the whipped topping. Spread the cream cheese mixture over the baked layer. Dissolve the gelatin in the boiling water in a heatproof bowl. Stir in the frozen strawberries. Let stand until partially set. Pour the gelatin mixture over the prepared layers. Chill, covered, until set.

Yield: *12 servings*

On January 22, 1996, Larry Carrier sold the speedway to Bruton Smith at a purchase price of $26 million. At the time of the sale, the facility seated 71,000.

Frozen Fruit Salad

1 teaspoon unflavored gelatin
2 tablespoons lemon juice
3 ounces cream cheese, softened
$^{1}/_{2}$ cup mayonnaise
$^{1}/_{8}$ teaspoon salt
$^{2}/_{3}$ cup whipping cream
$^{1}/_{2}$ cup sugar
2$^{1}/_{2}$ (15-ounce) cans fruit cocktail,
    drained
$^{1}/_{2}$ cup chopped pecans or walnuts

Soften the gelatin in the lemon juice in a small saucepan. Cook over low heat until the gelatin dissolves, stirring frequently. May use a double boiler. Combine the cream cheese, mayonnaise and salt in a bowl and mix until blended. Stir in the gelatin mixture.

Beat the whipping cream in a mixing bowl until soft peaks form. Add the sugar gradually, beating constantly until blended. Fold the cream cheese mixture, fruit cocktail and pecans into the whipped cream. Spoon into paper-lined muffin cups. Freeze, covered, for 4 to 6 hours or until set. Remove from the muffin tins to a plate. Thaw in the refrigerator for 30 minutes before serving. Serve on a lettuce-lined platter.

Yield: *10 to 12 servings*

Side by Side

Vegetables & Side Dishes

Chilled Asparagus with Herbed Yogurt Sauce

1 pound fresh asparagus
½ cup plain yogurt
2½ tablespoons (or less) Dijon
  mustard
2 tablespoons mayonnaise
1 tablespoon minced fresh dillweed
1 tablespoon minced fresh chives
⅛ teaspoon freshly ground pepper
Cherry tomatoes (optional)

Snap off the thick woody ends of the asparagus spears. Remove the scales with a knife if desired. Place the asparagus in a saucepan. Add just enough water to cover. Bring to a boil. Boil for 5 minutes or until tender-crisp; drain. Rinse with cold water and drain. Place the asparagus in a shallow dish. Chill, covered, in the refrigerator.

Combine the yogurt, Dijon mustard, mayonnaise, dillweed, chives and pepper in a bowl and mix well. Arrange the chilled asparagus on a lettuce-lined serving platter. Top with the yogurt sauce. Garnish with cherry tomatoes. Serve with beef or pork tenderloin.

Yield: *4 to 6 servings*

Roasted Asparagus

1 pound fresh medium asparagus
1 to 2 tablespoons olive oil
1 tablespoon lemon juice
½ teaspoon freshly ground pepper
⅛ to ¼ teaspoon salt

Snap off the thick woody ends of the asparagus spears. Arrange in a single layer in an ungreased 9×13-inch baking pan. Drizzle with the olive oil and lemon juice, turning to coat. Sprinkle with the pepper and salt and turn to coat.

Roast at 450 degrees for 15 to 20 minutes or until tender-crisp and light brown, turning once or twice during the roasting process. Serve hot or at room temperature.

Yield: *4 servings*

Best Times Baked Beans

Forget counting calories when you prepare this recipe!

1 pound bacon
4 Vidalia onions, chopped
2 (16-ounce) cans baked beans
1 (16-ounce) can baby butter beans,
  drained
1 (16-ounce) can grand yellow lima
  beans, drained
½ cup packed brown sugar
½ cup vinegar
2 tablespoons prepared yellow
  mustard
1 teaspoon garlic salt

Fry the bacon in a skillet until crisp. Remove the bacon with a slotted spoon to paper towels to drain, reserving 2 to 3 tablespoons of the pan drippings in the skillet. Crumble the bacon.

Sauté the onions in the reserved pan drippings until tender. Combine the bacon, sautéed onions, undrained baked beans, butter beans, lima beans, brown sugar, vinegar, prepared mustard and garlic salt in a bowl and mix well. Spoon the bean mixture into a 9×13-inch baking dish. Bake at 350 degrees for 30 to 45 minutes or until bubbly. For beans that are not as thick, do not drain the lima beans.

Yield: *10 to 12 servings*

By August of 1996, 15,000 seats had been added, bringing the seating capacity to 86,000.

Green Beans Caesar

1½ pounds fresh green beans,
    trimmed
2 tablespoons vegetable oil
1 tablespoon vinegar
1 tablespoon minced onion
1 garlic clove, crushed
¼ teaspoon salt
⅛ teaspoon pepper
2 tablespoons dry bread crumbs
2 tablespoons grated Parmesan
    cheese
1 tablespoon butter, melted
Paprika

Cut the beans into 1-inch pieces. Combine the beans with enough water to cover in a saucepan. Cook until tender-crisp; drain. Toss the beans with the oil, vinegar, onion, garlic, salt and pepper in a bowl. Spoon the bean mixture into an ungreased 1-quart baking dish.

Combine the bread crumbs, cheese and butter in a bowl and mix well. Sprinkle over the beans. Sprinkle with paprika. Bake at 350 degrees for 15 to 20 minutes or until heated through.

May substitute 2 drained 16-ounce cans cut green beans for the fresh green beans. Bake for 40 to 45 minutes or until heated through.

Yield: *6 servings*

Cowboy Beans

1 (16-ounce) can pork and beans
1 (16-ounce) can navy beans
1 (16-ounce) can butter beans
1 (16-ounce) can kidney beans
1 (28-ounce) can diced stewed
    tomatoes
2 cups barbecue sauce
1 medium onion, chopped
1 medium green bell pepper, chopped
2 pounds ground beef, browned,
    drained

Combine the undrained beans in a slow cooker and mix well. Stir in the undrained tomatoes and barbecue sauce. Add the onion, bell pepper and ground beef and mix well.

Cook on High for 2 hours, stirring occasionally. Reduce the setting to Low. Cook for 1 hour longer, stirring occasionally. Spoon into a serving bowl. May cook on the stovetop over low heat.

Yield: *12 to 15 servings*

Swiss Beans

1 (10-ounce) package frozen
    green beans
1/2 cup sour cream
2 tablespoons butter
1 teaspoon sugar
1/2 teaspoon salt
1/2 teaspoon grated onion
1/8 teaspoon pepper
1 cup shredded Swiss cheese
Paprika

Cook the green beans using package directions; drain. Stir in the sour cream, butter, sugar, salt, onion and pepper. Spoon the green bean mixture into a greased 1-quart baking dish. Sprinkle with the cheese and paprika. Bake at 350 degrees for 35 minutes.

Yield: *3 or 4 servings*

Broccoli Walnut Stir-Fry

1 large bunch broccoli
2 cups water
$\frac{1}{8}$ teaspoon salt
$\frac{1}{2}$ cup vegetable oil
$\frac{1}{2}$ cup walnut halves
2 tablespoons soy sauce
1 tablespoon sherry
$\frac{1}{2}$ teaspoon sugar

Discard the tough ends of the broccoli stems. Cut the broccoli into bite-size pieces. Bring the water and salt to a boil in a saucepan. Add the broccoli. Blanch for 2 minutes. Remove the broccoli to a bowl with a slotted spoon, reserving $\frac{1}{4}$ cup of the cooking water.

Heat the oil in a medium skillet or wok over medium-high heat. Add the walnuts. Fry for 1 minute. Remove the walnuts with a slotted spoon to a paper towel to drain, reserving the oil in the skillet.

Add the broccoli to the reserved oil. Cook for 1 to 2 minutes, stirring constantly. Stir in the reserved cooking water, soy sauce, sherry and sugar. Cook until bubbly, stirring frequently. Spoon into a serving bowl. Top with the walnuts. Serve immediately.

Yield: *4 servings*

Carrot Soufflé

1 pound carrots, peeled, sliced
½ cup (1 stick) butter, melted
3 eggs
¼ cup packed brown sugar
¼ cup sugar
3 tablespoons flour
1 teaspoon baking powder
½ teaspoon vanilla extract

Combine the carrots with enough water to cover in a saucepan. Bring to a boil. Boil until tender; drain. Combine the carrots and butter in a blender container. Process until smooth. Add the eggs, brown sugar, sugar, flour, baking powder and vanilla. Process until blended.

Spoon the carrot mixture into a lightly greased 1-quart baking dish. Bake at 350 degrees for 40 to 45 minutes or until brown and bubbly.

Yield: *6 servings*

Yummy Baked Carrots

1½ pounds fresh or frozen baby
      carrots
½ cup mayonnaise
2 tablespoons chopped onion
⅔ teaspoon horseradish
½ teaspoon salt
⅛ teaspoon pepper
7 butter crackers, crushed
2 tablespoons butter, melted

Cook, steam or microwave the carrots for 10 to 15 minutes or until tender-crisp; drain. Arrange the carrots in an ungreased 1-quart baking dish. Combine the mayonnaise, onion, horseradish, salt and pepper in a bowl and mix well. Spoon the mayonnaise mixture over the carrots. Top with a mixture of the cracker crumbs and butter.

Bake at 350 degrees for 30 minutes. This recipe may be doubled or tripled for large crowds.

Yield: *6 servings*

Corn Casserole

1 (16-ounce) can whole kernel corn,
    drained
1 (16-ounce) can cream-style corn
1 (8-ounce) package corn muffin mix
1 cup sour cream
1/2 cup (1 stick) margarine, melted
1 egg, beaten

Combine the whole kernel corn, cream-style corn, muffin mix, sour cream, margarine and egg in a bowl and mix well. Spoon the corn mixture into a 9×13-inch baking dish sprayed with nonstick cooking spray. Bake at 350 degrees for 1 hour or until set and light brown. Cut into squares to serve. Great with fish or barbecue.

Yield: *12 servings*

Grilled Corn

1/2 cup (1 stick) butter or margarine,
    softened
2 tablespoons snipped fresh chives
1 tablespoon lemon juice
4 ears of corn, husks and silk
    removed

Combine the butter, chives and lemon juice in a small bowl and mix well. Place each ear of corn on a sheet of heavy-duty foil. Spread the butter mixture over the entire surface of each ear of corn. Wrap securely with the foil. Grill the corn over hot coals for 15 to 20 minutes, turning every 5 minutes.

Yield: *4 servings*

Jamaican Corn

The photo for this recipe appears on the front cover.

10 ears of corn, husks and silk
    removed
2 zucchini, sliced
1 red onion, chopped
1 red bell pepper, chopped
½ cup (1 stick) butter, softened
Salt and pepper to taste

Combine the ears of corn with enough water to cover in a stockpot. Bring to a boil. Boil until tender; drain. Remove the kernels of the hot corn with a sharp knife into a microwave-safe bowl. Stir in the zucchini, onion and bell pepper. Add the butter and mix well. Season with salt and pepper. Microwave for 1 to 2 minutes or until the butter melts and the vegetables are tender-crisp.

Yield: *8 to 10 servings*

Dijon Herb Roasted Potatoes

2 pounds red potatoes, cut into
    chunks (about 6 medium
    potatoes)
5 tablespoons Dijon mustard
2 tablespoons olive oil
1 garlic clove, chopped
½ teaspoon Italian seasoning

Arrange the potatoes in a single layer in a lightly greased baking pan or on a baking sheet with sides. Combine the Dijon mustard, olive oil, garlic and Italian seasoning in a bowl and mix well. Drizzle the mustard mixture over the potatoes and turn to coat. Bake at 425 degrees for 35 to 40 minutes or until the potatoes are fork tender, turning occasionally.

Yield: *4 servings*

111

Golden Potato Casserole

Lynda Helton, wife of Mike Helton

1 (2-pound) package frozen hash
    brown potatoes
1 (10-ounce) can cream of
    chicken soup
10 ounces sharp Cheddar cheese,
    shredded
1 cup chopped onion
1 cup sour cream
1/2 cup (1 stick) butter, melted
1 teaspoon salt
1 teaspoon pepper
1 can French-fried onions

Combine the hash brown potatoes, soup, cheese, onion, sour cream, butter, salt and pepper in a bowl and mix well. Spoon into a baking dish sprayed with nonstick cooking spray. Top with the onions. Bake at 300 degrees for 1 hour.

Yield: *8 servings*

Spuds 'n' Cheese Bake

Lynn Bodine, wife of Todd Bodine

1 (10-ounce) can Cheddar cheese
    soup
1/3 cup sour cream or plain yogurt
1 green onion, chopped
Pepper to taste
3 cups seasoned stiff mashed cooked
    potatoes

Combine the soup, sour cream, green onion and pepper in a bowl and mix well. Stir in the potatoes. Spoon the potato mixture into a 1/2-quart baking dish sprayed with nonstick cooking spray. Bake at 350 degrees for 30 minutes or until heated through and light brown.

Yield: *8 servings*

Spinach Soufflé

1 tablespoon finely chopped onion
1 tablespoon butter
1½ tablespoons flour
1 cup milk
2 cups chopped cooked spinach,
 drained
½ cup shredded Cheddar cheese
Salt and pepper to taste
4 egg yolks
4 egg whites

Sauté the onion in the butter in a skillet until tender. Add the flour and mix well. Cook over low heat until bubbly, stirring constantly. Stir in the milk. Cook until thickened, stirring constantly. Add the spinach, cheese, salt and pepper and mix well. Cook until the cheese melts. Remove from heat. Let stand until cool. Whisk the egg yolks in a bowl until blended. Stir the egg yolks into the spinach mixture. Beat the egg whites in a mixing bowl until stiff peaks form. Fold the egg whites into the spinach mixture. Spoon the spinach mixture into a greased 2-quart baking dish. Bake at 350 degrees for 45 minutes.

Yield: *6 to 8 servings*

Confetti-Stuffed Acorn Squash

2 acorn squash
2 tablespoons butter
⅔ cup chopped leeks (white and
 light green parts only)
4 medium carrots, chopped
4 ribs celery, chopped
1 tablespoon minced gingerroot
2 tablespoons butter
¼ cup dry white wine
2 tablespoons soy sauce
1 cup shredded Monterey Jack cheese

Cut each squash through the stem into halves; discard the seeds. Rub the cut sides of the squash with 2 tablespoons butter. Arrange cut side down in a baking dish. Bake at 350 degrees for 25 minutes; turn. Bake for 15 minutes longer or until the squash is tender and easily pierced with a fork. Maintain the oven temperature. Sauté the leeks, carrots, celery and gingerroot in 2 tablespoons butter in a skillet until the leeks and carrots are tender. Stir in the wine and soy sauce. Bring to a boil. Boil until all of the liquid is absorbed, stirring frequently. Fill each squash half with some of the leek mixture. Sprinkle with the cheese. Bake for 6 to 8 minutes or until the cheese melts.

Yield: *4 servings*

Sweet Potatoes with Cranberries

3 (17-ounce) cans sweet potatoes
½ cup packed brown sugar
½ cup rolled oats
½ cup flour
1 tablespoon cinnamon
1 teaspoon nutmeg
⅓ cup margarine, softened
2 cups fresh cranberries (optional)
1½ cups miniature marshmallows

Mash the undrained sweet potatoes in a bowl. Combine the brown sugar, oats, flour, cinnamon and nutmeg in a bowl and mix well. Cut in the margarine until crumbly. Reserve 1 cup of the crumb mixture. Add the remaining crumb mixture to the sweet potatoes and mix well. Stir in the cranberries.

Spoon the sweet potato mixture into a greased 9×13-inch baking dish. Sprinkle with the reserved crumb mixture. Bake at 350 degrees for 30 minutes. Top with the marshmallows. Broil until golden brown.

Yield: *10 servings*

Root Vegetable Bake

2 turnips, peeled, thinly sliced
1 beet, peeled, thinly sliced
1 sweet potato, peeled, thinly sliced
1 baking potato, peeled, thinly sliced
2 carrots, peeled, thinly sliced
2 rutabagas, peeled, thinly sliced
2 teaspoons nutmeg
1 (12-ounce) can evaporated milk

Spray a 9×13-inch baking dish with nonstick cooking spray. Layer the turnips, beet, sweet potato, potato, carrots and rutabagas in the prepared baking dish, sprinkling ⅙ of the nutmeg and drizzling ¼ cup of the evaporated milk between each layer. Weight the baking dish with a heavy plate to compress the vegetables. Chill, covered, for 8 to 10 hours; remove the plate. Bake at 325 degrees for 30 to 40 minutes or until heated through.

Yield: *6 to 8 servings*

Roasted Rainbow Vegetables

2 medium russet potatoes, peeled,
    cut into 1-inch chunks
2 medium carrots, peeled, cut into
    1/2-inch slices
1 tablespoon olive oil
1 teaspoon basil, crushed
1 teaspoon oregano, crushed
1/4 teaspoon salt
1/4 teaspoon freshly ground pepper
1 large zucchini, cut into 1/2-inch
    slices
1 large red bell pepper, cut into
    1-inch chunks
2 garlic cloves, minced
2 cups shredded cheese

Arrange the potatoes and carrots in a single layer in a 9×13-inch baking dish. Drizzle with the olive oil. Sprinkle with the basil, oregano, salt and pepper and toss lightly to coat.

Bake at 425 degrees for 20 minutes. Add the zucchini, bell pepper and garlic and mix well. Bake for 20 minutes or until the vegetables are of the desired degree of tenderness. Sprinkle with the cheese. Bake for 2 minutes longer or just until the cheese melts.

Yield: *6 servings*

BMS continued to grow and by April of 1997 was the largest sports arena in Tennessee and one of the largest in the country, seating 118,000. The speedway also boasted 22 new skyboxes.

Lemon Couscous

1 cup chicken broth
2 tablespoons fresh lemon juice
1 tablespoon grated lemon zest
1 tablespoon butter
$1/8$ teaspoon salt
$2/3$ cup couscous
2 tablespoons pecan pieces, toasted
2 tablespoons chopped fresh parsley
2 tablespoons finely chopped red
    bell pepper
Sprigs of fresh mint (optional)
Lemon slices (optional)

Combine the broth, lemon juice, lemon zest, butter and salt in a saucepan. Bring to a boil over medium-high heat, stirring frequently. Add the couscous and mix well. Remove from heat.

Let stand, covered, for 10 minutes. Stir in the pecans, parsley and bell pepper. Spoon into a serving bowl. Garnish with sprigs of fresh mint and lemon slices.

Yield: *2 servings*

Baked Mushroom Rice

1 cup long grain rice
1 (10-ounce) can chicken broth
1 (10-ounce) can French onion soup
1 (2-ounce) jar sliced mushrooms,
    drained
1/4 cup (1/2 stick) butter or margarine,
    melted

Combine the rice, broth, soup, mushrooms and butter in a bowl and mix well. Spoon into an ungreased 2-quart baking dish. Bake, covered, at 350 degrees for 1 hour.

Yield: *4 servings*

Pineapple Casserole

3/4 cup sugar
1 tablespoon flour
2 (15-ounce) cans pineapple chunks,
    drained
1 cup shredded sharp Cheddar
    cheese
1 sleeve butter crackers, crumbled
1/2 cup (1 stick) butter, melted

Combine the sugar and flour in a bowl and mix well. Stir in the pineapple. Add the cheese and mix well. Spoon into a 7×11-inch baking dish sprayed with nonstick cooking spray. Sprinkle with the cracker crumbs. Drizzle with the butter. Bake at 325 degrees for 20 minutes.

Yield: *6 servings*

Grandstand

Gourmet

Sherried Beef

3 pounds stew beef, trimmed,
  cut into cubes
2 (10-ounce) cans cream of
  mushroom soup
1 (6-ounce) can mushrooms, drained
3/4 cup sherry
1/2 envelope onion soup mix
Hot cooked noodles, rice or mashed
  potatoes

Combine the stew beef, soup, mushrooms, sherry and onion soup mix in a bowl and mix well. Spoon into a baking dish sprayed with nonstick cooking spray.

Bake, covered, at 325 degrees for 3 hours or at 300 degrees for 4 hours or until the beef is tender. The 4-hour cooking time may require the addition of a small amount of water for the desired consistency. Serve over hot cooked noodles, rice or mashed potatoes.

Yield: *4 to 6 servings*

Busy Mom's Burger Cups

1 pound ground beef
1 (10-count) can buttermilk biscuits
1/2 cup barbecue sauce
1 cup shredded Cheddar cheese

Brown the ground beef in a skillet, stirring until crumbly; drain. Separate the biscuits. Pat each biscuit over the bottom and up the side of a greased muffin cup, allowing the side to hang over the edge.

Fill each biscuit cup with ground beef and a spoonful of the barbecue sauce. Sprinkle with the cheese. Bake at 350 degrees for 11 to 13 minutes or until golden brown.

Yield: *10 burger cups*

Family Race Night Taco Casserole

Nancy Andretti, wife of John Andretti

Family race night in downtown Bristol is pure excitement.
This is a great dinner to come home to.

1 pound lean ground beef
1 small onion, chopped
1 (8-ounce) can tomato sauce
1 envelope taco seasoning mix
½ teaspoon garlic powder
1 cup reduced-fat sour cream
1 cup reduced-fat cottage cheese
2 cups crushed tortilla chips
2 cups shredded Cheddar or
    Monterey Jack cheese

Brown the ground beef in a skillet, stirring until crumbly; drain. Stir in the onion, tomato sauce, seasoning mix and garlic powder. Remove from heat. Combine the sour cream and cottage cheese in a bowl and mix well.

Layer the tortilla chips, ground beef mixture, sour cream mixture and cheese ½ at a time in a 2½-quart baking dish sprayed with nonstick cooking spray. Bake at 350 degrees for 30 to 35 minutes or until brown and bubbly.

Yield: *4 servings*

For the August 1998 Goody's 500, the speedway featured more than 131,000 grandstand seats and 95 skyboxes.

Beef and Black Bean Pie

Debbie Benson, wife of Johnny Benson

1 pound lean ground beef
1 (15-ounce) can black beans,
    drained, rinsed
½ cup water
1 envelope taco seasoning mix
1 (8-ounce) package corn muffin mix
¾ cup shredded Cheddar cheese
¾ cup sour cream or light
    sour cream
½ cup sliced green onions
1 (8-ounce) can whole kernel corn,
    drained
¾ cup sour cream or light
    sour cream
¾ cup shredded Cheddar cheese
⅓ cup sliced green onions

Brown the ground beef in a skillet, stirring until crumbly; drain. Stir in the beans, water and seasoning mix. Bring to a boil; reduce heat. Simmer for 5 minutes, stirring occasionally. Remove from heat.

Combine the muffin mix, ¾ cup cheese, ¾ cup sour cream and ½ cup green onions in a bowl and mix just until moistened; batter will be stiff. Spread slightly more than half of the batter over the bottom and up the side of a 9-inch round baking dish using a spoon dipped in cold water. Layer the corn and the ground beef mixture over the prepared layer. Spoon the remaining batter along the outer edge, spreading as much as possible toward the center and leaving a 3-inch circle in the center uncovered.

Bake at 400 degrees for 20 to 25 minutes or until golden brown. Dollop ¾ cup sour cream on the top. Sprinkle with ¾ cup cheese and ⅓ cup green onions.

Yield: *4 or 5 servings*

Classic Spaghetti Pie

6 to 7 ounces spaghetti
2 tablespoons butter or margarine
1/3 cup grated Parmesan cheese
2 eggs, beaten
1 cup cottage cheese
1 pound ground beef
1/2 cup chopped onion
1/4 cup chopped green bell pepper
1 (8-ounce) can diced tomatoes
1 (6-ounce) can tomato paste
1 teaspoon sugar
1 teaspoon oregano, crushed
1/2 teaspoon garlic salt
1/2 cup shredded mozzarella cheese

Cook the pasta using package directions; drain. Add the butter and mix well. Stir in the Parmesan cheese and eggs. Pat the pasta mixture over the bottom and up the side of a buttered 10-inch pie plate to form a crust. Spread the cottage cheese over the bottom of the prepared layer.

Brown the ground beef with the onion and bell pepper in a skillet, stirring until the ground beef is crumbly and the vegetables are tender; drain. Stir in the undrained tomatoes, tomato paste, sugar, oregano and garlic salt. Cook until heated through, stirring occasionally.

Spoon the ground beef mixture into the prepared pie plate. Bake at 350 degrees for 20 minutes. Sprinkle with the mozzarella cheese. Bake for 5 minutes longer or until the cheese melts. Serve with a tossed green salad and garlic bread.

Yield: *6 servings*

Italian Meatballs

12 ounces ground beef
4 ounces hot pork sausage
½ cup soft bread crumbs
¼ cup milk
¼ cup grated Parmesan cheese
1 egg, beaten
2 tablespoons minced onion
1 teaspoon basil
½ teaspoon garlic powder
¼ teaspoon salt
¼ teaspoon pepper
1 (32-ounce) jar spaghetti sauce
Hot cooked spaghetti

Combine the ground beef, sausage, bread crumbs, milk, cheese, egg, onion, basil, garlic powder, salt and pepper in a bowl and mix well. Shape the ground beef mixture into 1-inch balls. Arrange the meatballs on a broiler rack in a broiler pan. Broil until cooked through, turning occasionally.

Transfer the meatballs to a large saucepan using a slotted spoon. Add the spaghetti sauce and mix well. Simmer for 10 minutes, stirring occasionally. Serve over hot cooked spaghetti.

For meatball subs, slice sub rolls horizontally into halves. Cover each roll half with 2 or 3 slices of provolone cheese. Cover bottom half with hot sliced meatballs and sauce. Arrange on a baking sheet. Bake at 350 degrees for 4 to 5 minutes or until the cheese melts. Sprinkle each sub with 2 tablespoons Parmesan cheese. Top with the sub roll tops.

Yield: *4 to 6 servings*

Italian Spaghetti Sauce

Meredith Bowman, mother of Ward and Jeff Burton

1¹/₂ pounds ground beef
1 large onion, chopped
1 green bell pepper, chopped
2 (28-ounce) cans tomatoes
4 (15-ounce) cans tomato sauce
2 tablespoons basil, or to taste
1 tablespoon sugar
1 tablespoon oregano, or to taste
2 teaspoons garlic powder, or to taste
³/₄ teaspoon salt, or to taste
¹/₂ teaspoon ground pepper, or to taste
¹/₂ teaspoon rosemary, or to taste

Brown the ground beef with the onion and
bell pepper in a Dutch oven, stirring until
the ground beef is crumbly; drain. Stir in the
undrained tomatoes, tomato sauce, basil, sugar,
oregano, garlic powder, salt, pepper and
rosemary. Simmer for several hours or until of
the desired consistency, stirring occasionally.
Taste and adjust the seasonings as desired. Serve
over hot cooked spaghetti.

Ward and Jeff love this spaghetti sauce, and I still
make it whenever they come home.

Yield: *6 to 8 servings*

"Big Orange" Pork Chops

6 pork chops, trimmed
½ cup orange juice
¼ cup packed dark brown sugar
1 teaspoon salt
½ teaspoon dry mustard
¼ teaspoon pepper

Arrange the pork chops in a roasting pan. Combine the orange juice, brown sugar, salt, dry mustard and pepper in a bowl and mix well. Pour over the pork chops. Bake at 350 degrees for 45 minutes, basting occasionally.

Yield: *6 servings*

Bristol Slow-Cooker Barbecue

2 small pork tenderloins, trimmed
¾ cup white vinegar
½ cup ketchup
½ cup water
3 tablespoons brown sugar
1 tablespoon hot pepper sauce
1 tablespoon minced onion
1 teaspoon salt
1 teaspoon pepper
1 teaspoon paprika

Cut the pork into 2- to 3-inch slices. Combine the pork, vinegar, ketchup, water, brown sugar, hot pepper sauce, onion, salt, pepper and paprika in a slow cooker and mix well. Cook on High for 3 hours; reduce setting to Low. Cook for 3 to 4 hours longer or until the pork is tender, adding additional water if needed for the desired consistency. Open the slow cooker no more than is necessary during the cooking process.

To serve, mound the barbecue onto soft sandwich rolls with a slotted spoon. Top with coleslaw if desired. Also good served as an entrée with potatoes, rice or baked beans.

Yield: *10 servings*

Ham and Cheddar Potato Gratin

This is a delicious way to use leftover ham.

6 medium russet potatoes, peeled,
   sliced
1½ cups cubed cooked ham
3 tablespoons butter
3 tablespoons flour
1 teaspoon dry mustard
½ teaspoon onion powder
¼ teaspoon salt
⅛ teaspoon ground white pepper
2 cups milk
1½ cups shredded Cheddar cheese
1 cup dry bread crumbs
1 tablespoon butter, melted

Combine the potatoes with enough water to cover in a saucepan. Bring to a boil. Remove from heat immediately; drain. Combine the potatoes and ham in a greased 2-quart oval baking dish and mix gently.

Heat 3 tablespoons butter in a saucepan until melted. Stir in the flour, dry mustard, onion powder, salt and white pepper. Cook over low heat until the mixture begins to bubble, stirring constantly. Remove from heat. Add the milk gradually, stirring constantly. Bring to a boil, stirring constantly. Cook until thickened, stirring constantly. Add the cheese. Cook until the cheese melts, stirring constantly.

Pour the cheese sauce over the potato mixture. Combine the bread crumbs and 1 tablespoon butter in a bowl and mix well. Sprinkle the bread crumb mixture over the top. Bake at 350 degrees for 30 to 35 minutes or until brown and bubbly.

Yield: *4 to 6 servings*

Chicken Extravaganza

1 (4- to 6-ounce) jar dried chipped
    beef
6 to 8 boneless skinless
    chicken breasts
6 to 8 slices bacon (optional)
1 (10-ounce) can cream of mushroom
    soup
1 cup sour cream
1 (4-ounce) can sliced mushrooms,
    drained
1 tablespoon Worcestershire sauce

Spray a 9×13-inch baking dish with nonstick cooking spray. Line the bottom of the prepared dish with the chipped beef. Wrap each chicken breast with a slice of bacon. Arrange the chicken breasts in a single layer over the chipped beef.

Combine the soup, sour cream, mushrooms and Worcestershire sauce in a bowl and mix well. Spoon over the chicken. Bake at 300 degrees for 2½ to 3 hours or until the chicken is cooked through. May prepare in advance and store, covered, in the refrigerator until just before baking.

Yield: *6 to 8 servings*

Special Chicken

1 cup sour cream
2 teaspoons lemon juice
2 teaspoons Worcestershire sauce
1 teaspoon paprika
1 teaspoon garlic powder
1 teaspoon celery salt
½ teaspoon salt
½ teaspoon pepper
8 to 12 boneless skinless
    chicken breasts
1 (8-ounce) package herb-seasoned
    stuffing mix, crushed
½ cup (1 stick) butter, melted

Combine the sour cream, lemon juice, Worcestershire sauce, paprika, garlic powder, celery salt, salt and pepper in a bowl and mix well. Coat the chicken with the sour cream mixture. Arrange the chicken in a single layer in a dish. Chill, covered, for 8 to 12 hours.

Coat the chicken with the stuffing mix. Arrange the chicken in a single layer in a 9×13-inch baking dish sprayed with nonstick cooking spray. Drizzle with the butter. Bake at 325 degrees for 1½ hours or until the chicken is cooked through.

Yield: *8 to 12 servings*

128

Home-Style Slow-Cooker Chicken

6 boneless skinless chicken breasts,
    cut into thirds
Salt to taste
Paprika to taste
½ cup (1 stick) butter
1 small onion, finely chopped
¼ teaspoon garlic powder
1 cup sliced mushrooms
¼ cup flour
1 tablespoon sugar
2 cups chicken bouillon
2 tablespoons lemon juice

Season the chicken with salt and paprika. Brown the chicken on both sides in ¼ cup of the butter in a skillet. Transfer the chicken to a slow cooker with a slotted spoon, reserving the pan drippings in the skillet.

Add the remaining ¼ cup butter to the reserved pan drippings. Stir in the onion and garlic powder. Cook over low heat for 5 minutes, stirring occasionally. Add the mushrooms and mix well. Cook for 2 minutes longer, stirring frequently. Stir in the flour and sugar. Add the bouillon and lemon juice and mix well.

Cook until thickened, stirring occasionally. Pour the sauce over the chicken. Cook, covered, on Low for 8 hours or on High for 3 hours.

You may add an additional ¼ cup bouillon or water during the cooking process for a thinner consistency. Serve with hot cooked egg noodles and buttered carrots.

Yield: *6 servings*

The seating capacity for 2000 reached 147,000 with the completion of the Kulwicki Terrace and Kulwicki Tower addition.

Fast-Track Fiesta Chicken Bake

5 or 6 boneless skinless chicken
    breasts, trimmed
3 quarts water
Salt to taste
1 (10-ounce) can 98% fat-free cream
    of chicken soup
1 (7-ounce) can mild salsa verde
1 cup nonfat sour cream
1 (8-ounce) package bite-size baked
    tortilla chips
8 ounces shredded Mexican cheese

Combine the chicken, water and salt in a large saucepan. Bring to a boil. Boil for 20 minutes. Drain, reserving ½ cup of the cooking liquid. Shred the chicken using 2 forks.

Combine the soup, salsa verde and sour cream in a saucepan and mix well. Cook over medium heat until heated through, stirring occasionally. Stir in the reserved cooking liquid.

Spray a 9×13-inch baking dish with nonstick cooking spray. Line the bottom of the prepared dish in a single layer with 24 of the tortilla chips. Layer the chicken, soup mixture and cheese ½ at a time in the prepared baking dish. Crush the remaining chips and sprinkle over the top. Bake, covered with foil, at 350 degrees for 20 minutes; remove the foil. Bake for 10 to 15 minutes longer or until bubbly and just beginning to brown. Serve with hot cooked rice and a tossed green salad or corn and black bean salad.

You may substitute 4 cups shredded cooked chicken parts for the chicken breasts and a mixture of 1 cup shredded sharp Cheddar cheese and 1 cup shredded Monterey Jack cheese for the Mexican cheese.

Yield: *6 to 8 servings*

Creamy Chicken Enchiladas

4 or 5 boneless skinless
    chicken breasts
Salt to taste
1 medium onion, chopped
1 tablespoon butter
1 (4-ounce) can chopped green chiles,
    drained
8 ounces cream cheese, chopped
8 (8-inch) flour tortillas
2 cups shredded Monterey Jack
    cheese
2 cups whipping cream

Combine the chicken and salt with enough water to cover in a saucepan. Bring to a boil. Boil for 20 minutes; drain. Chop the chicken into ½-inch pieces. Sauté the onion in the butter in a skillet until tender. Stir in the chicken and green chiles. Add the cream cheese. Cook over medium heat until the cream cheese melts, stirring constantly. Spoon ¼ cup of the chicken mixture down the center of each tortilla. Roll to enclose the filling. Arrange seam side down in a 9×13-inch baking dish. Sprinkle with the Monterey Jack cheese and drizzle with the whipping cream. Bake at 350 degrees for 25 to 35 minutes or until bubbly. You may substitute 3½ cups chopped cooked chicken for the chicken breasts.

Yield: *8 enchiladas*

Quick Oven Chicken and Dumplings

5 boneless skinless chicken breasts,
    cooked, chopped
½ cup (1 stick) butter, melted
1 cup baking mix
1 cup milk
2 cups chicken broth
1 (10-ounce) can cream of chicken
    soup
Paprika to taste

Arrange the chicken in a 9×12-inch baking dish sprayed with nonstick cooking spray. Drizzle with the butter. Sprinkle with the baking mix and pour the milk over the top. Combine the broth and soup in a bowl and mix well. Spoon the soup mixture over the prepared layers. Sprinkle with paprika. Bake at 350 degrees for 45 minutes. Let stand for 5 to 8 minutes before serving.

Yield: *4 servings*

Chicken and Wild Rice Casserole

1 (6-ounce) package long grain and
    wild rice mix
$2^1/3$ cups chicken broth
3 cups chopped cooked chicken
2 (16-ounce) cans French-style green
    beans, drained
1 (10-ounce) can cream of celery soup
1 (8-ounce) can water chestnuts,
    drained, sliced
1 cup mayonnaise
1 medium onion, chopped
Salt and pepper to taste
Paprika to taste
Chopped fresh parsley

Prepare the rice using package directions and substituting the broth for the liquid. Combine the rice, chicken, green beans, soup, water chestnuts, mayonnaise and onion in a bowl and mix well. Season with salt and pepper. Spoon the chicken mixture into a 3-quart baking dish sprayed with nonstick cooking spray. Sprinkle with paprika and parsley. Bake at 350 degrees for 30 to 45 minutes or until heated through.

Yield: *8 servings*

William and Mary Chicken Casserole

2 (10-ounce) packages frozen
    broccoli
2 cups sliced cooked chicken
2 (10-ounce) cans cream of chicken
    soup
1 cup mayonnaise
1 teaspoon lemon juice
$1/2$ teaspoon curry powder
$1/2$ cup shredded sharp Cheddar
    cheese
$1/2$ cup soft bread crumbs
1 tablespoon butter, melted

Cook the broccoli using package directions until tender; drain. Arrange the broccoli in a greased 7×11-inch baking dish. Top with the chicken.

Combine the soup, mayonnaise, lemon juice and curry powder in a bowl and mix well. Spread over the chicken. Sprinkle with the cheese. Top with a mixture of the bread crumbs and butter. Bake at 350 degrees for 25 to 30 minutes or until heated through.

Yield: *6 to 8 servings*

King Ranch Casserole

3 to 4 cups chopped cooked chicken
1 medium onion, chopped
1 (10-ounce) can cream of mushroom
    soup
1 (10-ounce) can cream of chicken
    soup
1 (10-ounce) can tomatoes with
    green chiles
1 cup chicken broth
Cayenne pepper to taste
12 corn tortillas, cut into quarters
1½ teaspoons chili powder
Garlic salt to taste
3 cups shredded sharp Cheddar
    cheese

Combine the chicken and onion in a bowl and mix well. Combine the soups, undrained tomatoes, broth and cayenne pepper in a bowl and mix well.

Layer the tortillas, chicken mixture and soup mixture ½ at a time in a 9×13-inch baking dish sprayed with nonstick cooking spray. Sprinkle with chili powder and garlic salt. Top with the cheese. Bake at 350 degrees for 30 to 40 minutes or until bubbly. Serve with tortilla chips and pinto beans.

Yield: *6 to 8 servings*

Rusty Wallace snapped Jeff Gordon's four-year Food City 500 winning streak in 1999.

Chicken Spaghetti

Ann Schrader, wife of Ken Schrader

This is Ken Schrader's favorite entrée.

8 to 10 boneless skinless
    chicken breasts
3 quarts water
Salt and pepper to taste
16 ounces vermicelli
2 pounds Velveeta cheese, chopped
1 (14-ounce) can tiny peas, drained
1 (10-ounce) can tomatoes with
    green chiles
1 (8-ounce) jar sliced mushrooms,
    drained
8 large carrots, peeled, chopped
2 tablespoons Worcestershire sauce
2 large green bell peppers, chopped
2 large onions, chopped
¼ cup (½ stick) butter

Combine the chicken, water, salt and pepper in a stockpot. Bring to a boil. Boil until the chicken is tender. Remove the chicken to a platter with a slotted spoon, reserving the broth. Chop the chicken into bite-size pieces.

Cook the pasta in the reserved broth until tender, adding the chicken, cheese, peas, undrained tomatoes, mushrooms, carrots and Worcestershire sauce during the cooking process and stirring occasionally.

Sauté the bell peppers and onions in the butter in a skillet until tender. Add the bell pepper mixture to the chicken mixture and mix well. Spoon the chicken mixture into two 9×12-inch baking dishes sprayed with nonstick cooking spray. Bake at 350 degrees for 45 minutes or until bubbly. You may freeze for future use.

Yield: *12 to 16 servings*

Chicken and Shrimp Jambalaya

8 ounces bulk sausage
1 cup sliced celery
1 cup chopped green bell pepper
1 cup chopped onion
2 garlic cloves, finely chopped
1 (28-ounce) can whole tomatoes
3 cups water
2 cups chopped cooked chicken
¾ cup long grain rice
4 teaspoons chicken bouillon
　　granules, or 4 chicken
　　bouillon cubes
½ teaspoon paprika
½ teaspoon black pepper
¼ teaspoon cayenne pepper
¼ teaspoon thyme
8 ounces medium shrimp, peeled

Brown the sausage in a Dutch oven, stirring until crumbly. Add the celery, bell pepper, onion and garlic. Cook until the vegetables are tender, stirring frequently. Stir in the undrained tomatoes, water, chicken, rice, bouillon granules, paprika, black pepper, cayenne pepper and thyme. Bring to a boil; reduce heat.

Simmer, covered, for 30 minutes, stirring occasionally. Add the shrimp and mix well. Cook, covered, for 5 minutes longer or until the shrimp turn pink, stirring occasionally. Serve with hot pepper sauce.

Yield: *4 quarts*

Skybox Dining

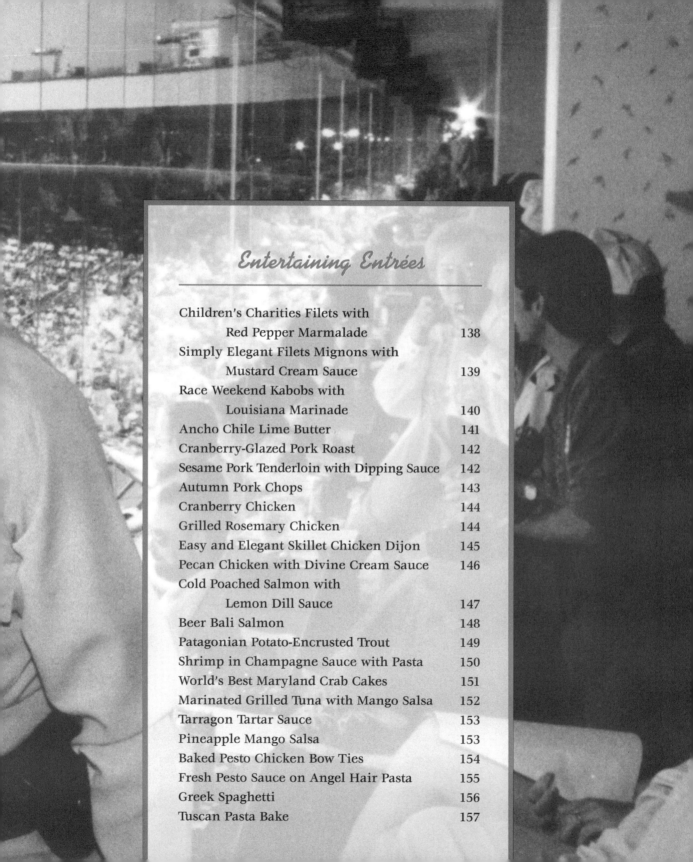

Entertaining Entrées

Children's Charities Filets with Red Pepper Marmalade

The Centre located in Bristol, Tennessee, contributed this recipe.

Red Pepper Marmalade
1/4 cup olive oil
1 tablespoon butter
1 ounce fresh gingerroot, minced
3 garlic cloves, minced
4 large red bell peppers, thinly sliced
Zest of 1 orange
1/4 cup fresh orange juice
1 tablespoon sugar
1/2 teaspoon ground pepper

For the marmalade, heat the olive oil, butter, gingerroot and garlic in a skillet over medium heat for 3 minutes, stirring frequently. Add the bell peppers, orange zest, orange juice, sugar and pepper and mix well. Cook over very low heat for 1 to 1 1/4 hours or until the liquid evaporates, stirring frequently; do not allow to blacken. The marmalade may be prepared 1 day in advance and stored, covered, in the refrigerator. Reheat before serving.

Filets Mignons
4 (6-ounce) filets mignons
Olive oil to taste
Salt and pepper to taste

For the filets, rub the surface of the filets lightly with olive oil. Sprinkle with salt and pepper. Grill over hot coals for 3 to 5 minutes per side or until of the desired degree of doneness. Arrange the filets on a serving platter. Top each with some of the marmalade.

Yield: *4 servings*

BMS' Fantasy in Lights, celebrating its fourth season this year, raised more than $350,000 in its first three seasons for local charities through Bristol's Chapter of Speedway Children's Charities.

Simply Elegant Filets Mignons with Mustard Cream Sauce

Diane Green, wife of David Green

1½ teaspoons butter
1½ teaspoons vegetable oil
Freshly ground pepper
2 filets mignons, 1¼ inches thick
Salt to taste
1½ teaspoons butter
1 shallot, minced
1 tablespoon brandy
⅓ cup whipping cream
½ teaspoon Dijon mustard
Sprigs of fresh parsley

Heat 1½ teaspoons butter and oil in a medium heavy skillet over high heat. Grind the pepper generously over both sides of the filets and press lightly. Sprinkle salt on 1 side of the filets. Arrange the filets salt side down in the butter mixture. Cook for 2 minutes or until brown. Sprinkle with salt and turn. Cook until brown. Reduce the heat to medium.

Cook for 6 minutes longer for rare or until of the desired degree of doneness, turning occasionally. Remove the filets to heated dinner plates.

Discard the pan drippings from the skillet. Add 1½ teaspoons butter to the skillet and heat over medium heat. Stir in the shallot. Cook for 1 minute, stirring constantly. Remove from heat. Stir in the brandy. Return the skillet to the heat. Add the whipping cream and mix well. Stir in the Dijon mustard. Cook just until heated through, stirring frequently. Drizzle over the filets. Garnish with parsley.

Yield: *2 servings*

Race Weekend Kabobs with Louisiana Marinade

The photo for this recipe appears on the cover.

Louisiana Marinade
2 cups red wine
1½ cups olive oil
½ cup soy sauce
¼ cup Worcestershire sauce
2 medium onions, chopped
2 garlic cloves, minced
2 tablespoons dry mustard
1 tablespoon black pepper
1½ teaspoons parsley
¼ teaspoon salt
¼ teaspoon cayenne pepper

For the marinade, combine the wine, olive oil, soy sauce, Worcestershire sauce, onions, garlic, dry mustard, black pepper, parsley, salt and cayenne pepper in a bowl and mix well. Great marinade for game and leaner cuts of beef such as London broil, flank steak or round steak.

Kabobs
2 pounds top sirloin, cut into
    1½-inch pieces
18 to 24 cherry tomatoes
¼ cup sliced scallions

For the kabobs, pour the marinade over the beef in a shallow dish and toss to coat. Marinate, covered, in the refrigerator for 4 to 8 hours, stirring occasionally; drain.

Thread the beef and cherry tomatoes alternately on 8 metal skewers or 8 wooden skewers that have been soaked in water for 30 minutes. Brush the grill rack with oil. Grill the kabobs over medium heat for 7 to 8 minutes or until the beef is of the desired degree of doneness and the tomatoes are lightly charred, turning once. Thread the scallion slices on the ends of the skewers before serving.

You may substitute vegetables of your choice, such as green or red bell peppers, onions or mushrooms, for some of the cherry tomatoes.

Yield: *8 servings*

Ancho Chile Lime Butter

Country Club of Bristol located in Bristol, Tennessee, contributed this recipe. Use this butter on grilled or broiled meats, seafood, corn on the cob, baked or mashed potatoes, pasta, or other vegetables.

3 dried ancho chile pods
Grated zest and juice of 2 limes
3 garlic cloves, minced
1 teaspoon cumin
1/2 teaspoon cayenne pepper
  (optional)
Kosher salt to taste
2 cups (4 sticks) unsalted butter,
  softened

Remove the seeds from the chiles and discard. Soak the chiles in enough warm water to cover in a bowl until softened. Drain, reserving the liquid for other uses if desired.

Combine the chiles, lime zest, lime juice, garlic, cumin, cayenne pepper and kosher salt in a food processor container. Process until of a paste consistency. Combine the chile paste with the butter in a bowl and mix well. Shape the butter mixture into a log. Chill, tightly wrapped in plastic wrap, until firm. Cut into 1/2-inch slices as needed.

Yield: *1 pound ancho chile lime butter*

The qualifying record for BMS is 126,370 (15,184 sec.) set by Steve Park (Chevrolet) on March 26, 2000. The race record is 101.074 set on July 11, 1971, by Charlie Glotzbach.

Cranberry-Glazed Pork Roast

2 teaspoons cornstarch
¼ teaspoon cinnamon
⅛ teaspoon salt
1 (16-ounce) can whole cranberry
    sauce
2 tablespoons sherry
2 tablespoons orange juice
½ teaspoon grated orange zest
1 (4-pound) boneless pork loin roast

Combine the cornstarch, cinnamon and salt in a saucepan and mix well. Stir in the cranberry sauce, sherry, orange juice and orange zest. Cook until thickened, stirring frequently. Place the roast in a baking pan. Roast at 350 degrees for 45 minutes. Spoon half the cranberry sauce over the roast. Roast until a meat thermometer registers 160 degrees. Remove the roast to a serving platter. Serve with the remaining cranberry sauce.

Yield: *12 servings*

Sesame Pork Tenderloin with Dipping Sauce

Pork Tenderloin
1½ pounds pork tenderloin
⅓ cup cooking sherry
1 tablespoon soy sauce
½ cup honey
½ cup sesame seeds

For the tenderloin, place the tenderloin in a sealable plastic bag. Pour a mixture of the sherry and soy sauce over the tenderloin. Seal tightly and toss to coat. Marinate in the refrigerator for 1 hour, turning several times. Spread the honey on a plate. Spread the sesame seeds in a shallow dish. Roll the tenderloin in the honey and then in the sesame seeds. Arrange the tenderloin on a roasting rack in a roasting pan. Roast at 350 degrees for 1 hour. Let stand for 10 minutes.

Dipping Sauce
⅓ cup soy sauce
1 tablespoon dry sherry
1 tablespoon sesame oil
1 green onion, finely chopped
1 garlic clove, crushed
½ teaspoon freshly grated gingerroot

For the sauce, combine the soy sauce, sherry, sesame oil, green onion, garlic and gingerroot in a small bowl and mix well.

To serve, place the sauce in the center of a serving platter. Surround the bowl with fresh spinach. Cut the tenderloin diagonally into thin slices. Arrange the slices over the spinach.

Yield: *10 to 12 servings*

142

Autumn Pork Chops

2½ teaspoons salt
2 teaspoons sage
4 pork chops, ½ inch thick
1 tablespoon vegetable oil
3 tablespoons flour
1 cup warm water
½ cup raisins
1 tablespoon cider vinegar
3 unpeeled Granny Smith apples,
    sliced
3 tablespoons molasses

Combine the salt and sage in a small bowl and mix well. Sprinkle the salt mixture on both sides of the pork chops. Heat the oil in a cast-iron skillet. Add the pork chops. Cook until brown on both sides, turning once. Remove the pork chops to a plate with a slotted spoon, reserving the pan drippings in the skillet.

Stir the flour into the reserved pan drippings. Cook until brown, stirring constantly. Add the warm water and mix well. Bring to a boil. Stir in the raisins and vinegar. Return the pork chops to the skillet. Top the pork chops with the sliced apples. Drizzle with the molasses. Bake, covered, at 350 degrees for 40 to 45 minutes or until the pork chops are cooked through.

Yield: *4 servings*

In June of 2000, BMSD unloaded more than 1400 truckloads of dirt over its famous high banks to host two weekends of dirt racing with the Hav-A-Tampa series and the World of Outlaws. The first Tractor Pull was featured in September 2000 using some of the same dirt.

Cranberry Chicken

Karl P. Harris, executive chef at the Brooklyn Grill in Bristol, Virginia, contributed this recipe.

1 (7-ounce) boneless skinless
    chicken breast
1/3 cup seasoned cracker meal
Salt and pepper to taste
1 teaspoon butter
2 ounces mozzarella cheese, sliced
3 ounces canned cranberry sauce,
    heated

Coat the chicken with a mixture of the cracker meal, salt and pepper. Sauté the chicken in the butter in a skillet for 2 minutes or until golden brown on both sides.

Arrange the chicken in a baking dish. Bake at 375 degrees for 7 to 10 minutes or until cooked through. Top with the mozzarella cheese. Bake for 1 to 2 minutes longer or until the cheese melts. Drizzle with the cranberry sauce. Serve with steamed red bliss potatoes and steamed green beans.

Yield: *1 serving*

Grilled Rosemary Chicken

8 to 12 boneless skinless chicken
    breasts
1 (16-ounce) bottle Italian salad
    dressing
1/2 cup dry white wine
1/4 cup soy sauce
1/4 cup (rounded) packed brown sugar
2 teaspoons rosemary
1 teaspoon salt
1 teaspoon pepper

Place the chicken in a deep plastic or glass bowl or a large sealable plastic bag. Combine the salad dressing, wine, soy sauce, brown sugar, rosemary, salt and pepper in a bowl and mix well. Pour over the chicken, turning to coat. Marinate, covered, in the refrigerator for 8 to 10 hours, turning occasionally.

Drain the chicken, reserving the marinade. Grill over hot coals until the chicken is cooked through, turning and basting with the reserved marinade occasionally.

Yield: *8 to 12 servings*

144

Easy and Elegant Skillet Chicken Dijon

¹/₃ cup flour
1 teaspoon thyme
¹/₂ teaspoon salt
¹/₄ teaspoon red pepper
4 boneless skinless chicken breasts,
*   or 4 thin loin pork chops*
6 tablespoons unsalted butter
1 cup sliced fresh mushrooms
4 shallots, finely chopped
³/₄ cup dry white wine
2 tablespoons Dijon mustard
³/₄ cup heavy cream or buttermilk
Paprika to taste

Combine the flour, thyme, salt and red pepper in a shallow dish and mix well. Coat both sides of the chicken with the flour mixture.

Heat 3 tablespoons of the butter in a large skillet over medium heat. Add the chicken. Cook until cooked through and light brown on both sides. Remove the chicken to an ovenproof platter with a slotted spoon, reserving the pan drippings in the skillet. Cover the chicken with foil and place in a 200-degree oven to keep warm.

Add the remaining 3 tablespoons butter to the reserved pan drippings. Heat over medium heat. Add the mushrooms and shallots and mix well. Sauté until the shallots are tender. Add the wine and stir to dislodge any browned bits. Cook for 1 to 2 minutes, stirring constantly. Add the Dijon mustard and mix well. Stir in the cream. Cook for 6 to 8 minutes or until reduced by half, stirring constantly. Drizzle over the chicken. Sprinkle with paprika. Serve immediately.

Yield: *4 servings*

Pecan Chicken with Divine Cream Sauce

1 cup flour
1 cup crushed pecans
1 teaspoon thyme
1 teaspoon basil
Salt and black pepper to taste
1/2 cup water
1/2 cup milk
1 egg
Hot pepper sauce to taste
1/2 cup vegetable oil
6 boneless skinless chicken breasts
1/4 cup crushed pecans
1/4 cup Frangelico
2 cups heavy cream

Combine the flour, 1 cup pecans, thyme, basil, salt and black pepper in a bowl and mix well. Whisk the water, milk and egg in a bowl until blended. Season with salt, black pepper and hot pepper sauce.

Heat the oil in a large heavy skillet over medium-high heat. Dip the chicken in the egg mixture. Coat with the flour mixture, shaking off the excess. Pan-fry the chicken in the hot oil for 15 to 17 minutes or until golden brown and cooked through, turning once. Remove the chicken to a heated platter with a slotted spoon, reserving the pan drippings. Tent the chicken with foil to keep warm.

Drain the pan drippings, reserving 1 tablespoon in the skillet. Sauté 1/4 cup pecans in the reserved pan drippings for 1 minute. Transfer the pecans to a bowl. Remove the skillet from the heat. Deglaze the skillet with the liqueur, stirring to dislodge any browned bits. Return the skillet to the heat. Stir in the cream. Bring to a boil; reduce heat. Simmer until reduced by 1/2, stirring frequently. Season with salt and black pepper.

Arrange 1 chicken breast on each of 6 serving plates. Drizzle each with about 1/4 cup of the sauce. Sprinkle with the sautéed pecans.

Yield: *6 servings*

Cold Poached Salmon with Lemon Dill Sauce

Serve as an entrée or as an appetizer with assorted party crackers.

Salmon
2 quarts water
1 medium onion, sliced
¼ cup fresh lemon juice
10 whole black peppercorns
2 teaspoons salt
2 bay leaves
6 salmon steaks, 1 inch thick

For the salmon, bring the water, onion, lemon juice, peppercorns, salt and bay leaves to a boil in a large heavy saucepan; reduce heat. Simmer, covered, for 30 minutes. Add 3 of the steaks. Simmer for 6 minutes or just until cooked through. Transfer the steaks to a plate with a slotted spoon. Repeat the process with the remaining steaks. Chill, covered, for 2 hours. The flavor is enhanced if prepared 1 day in advance and chilled, covered, for 8 to 10 hours.

Lemon Dill Sauce
1 cup mayonnaise
¼ cup buttermilk
2 tablespoons chopped fresh dillweed,
    or 2 teaspoons dried dillweed
1 tablespoon minced fresh parsley
2 teaspoons fresh lemon juice
1 small garlic clove, crushed

For the sauce, combine the mayonnaise, buttermilk, dillweed, parsley, lemon juice and garlic in a bowl and mix well. Chill, covered, for 1 hour or longer. Serve with the salmon.

Yield: *6 servings*

Beer Bali Salmon

6 (6- to 8-ounce) salmon fillets or
  steaks
³/₄ cup beer
¹/₂ cup orange marmalade
¹/₂ cup soy sauce
3 tablespoons sugar
2 tablespoons canola or vegetable oil
2 teaspoons minced fresh garlic
1 teaspoon minced gingerroot
2 or 3 green onions, sliced

Place the salmon in a large sealable plastic bag. Combine the beer, marmalade, soy sauce, sugar, canola oil, garlic and gingerroot in a bowl and mix well. Pour over the salmon and seal tightly. Turn to coat. Marinate in the refrigerator for 1 to 3 hours, turning occasionally.

Drain, reserving 1 cup of the marinade. Arrange the salmon in a single layer in a 9×13-inch baking dish sprayed with nonstick cooking spray. Pour the reserved marinade over the salmon. Bake at 350 degrees for 20 minutes or until the salmon flakes easily and is opaque. Remove the salmon to a serving platter. Sprinkle with the green onions.

To grill the salmon, arrange the fillets or steaks on a large sheet of heavy-duty foil and bend the edges of the foil. Drizzle with a small amount of the reserved marinade. Grill with lid down and vents open over medium-high heat until the salmon flakes easily.

Yield: *6 servings*

Patagonian Potato-Encrusted Trout

The Tavern, located in Abingdon, Virginia, contributed this recipe. Trout is a staple in Patagonia and is often served with potatoes. Trout fishing in local rivers is a great way to relax after an exciting race weekend.

1 pound baking potatoes, peeled
Salt and freshly ground pepper
*   to taste*
2 rainbow trout fillets, skinned
Grated zest and juice of 1 lemon
¼ cup (½ stick) unsalted butter
1 tablespoon (about) vegetable oil
10 fresh spinach leaves, stems
*   removed*

Combine the potatoes with enough water to cover in a saucepan. Bring to a boil. Boil for 15 minutes or until the outside of the potatoes are tender but the centers are hard; drain. Let stand until cool. Coarsely grate the potatoes into a bowl. Season with salt and pepper and mix well.

Sprinkle both sides of the fillets with salt, pepper and lemon zest. Drizzle with the lemon juice. Heat the butter and oil in a sauté pan over medium heat until the butter melts. Spoon ½ cup of the potato mixture into the center of the pan and flatten into a circle. Top with 1 of the fillets. Cover with half the spinach leaves and top with ½ cup of the potato mixture.

Cook until the potatoes are golden brown; turn carefully. Cook until golden brown. Remove to a paper towel to drain. Sprinkle with salt and pepper. Repeat the process with the remaining potato mixture, remaining fillet and remaining spinach leaves. Sprinkle with salt and pepper and serve immediately.

Yield: *2 servings*

Shrimp in Champagne Sauce with Pasta

1 pound medium shrimp, peeled,
 deveined
1½ cups Champagne
¼ teaspoon salt
2 tablespoons chopped scallions
2 plum tomatoes, chopped
¾ cup heavy cream
Salt and pepper to taste
16 ounces angel hair pasta
¼ cup heavy cream
3 tablespoons chopped fresh parsley,
 or 1 tablespoon parsley flakes

Combine the shrimp, Champagne and ¼ teaspoon salt in a saucepan. Cook over high heat until the liquid comes to a boil. Remove the shrimp with a slotted spoon to a bowl, reserving the liquid. Add the scallions and tomatoes to the reserved liquid. Bring to a boil. Boil for 8 minutes or until the liquid is reduced to ½ cup, stirring occasionally. Add ¾ cup cream and mix well.

Boil for 1 to 2 minutes or until slightly thickened, stirring occasionally. Return the shrimp to the saucepan. Cook just until heated through, stirring frequently. Taste and season with salt and pepper.

Cook the pasta using package directions; drain. Toss the pasta with ¼ cup cream and parsley in a bowl until coated. Spoon the pasta onto a serving platter. Top with the shrimp mixture.

Yield: *4 servings*

World's Best Maryland Crab Cakes

1 pound fresh lump crab meat,
 shells removed
2 slices bread, crusts removed
Milk
1 tablespoon mayonnaise
1 tablespoon parsley flakes
1 tablespoon baking powder
1 teaspoon Old Bay seasoning
1 egg, beaten
3/4 sleeve butter crackers, crushed
Canola oil

Place the crab meat in a bowl. Tear the bread into 1/2-inch pieces and place in a small bowl. Moisten with a few drops of milk. Squeeze the milk from the bread and add the bread to the crab meat and mix well. Add the mayonnaise, parsley flakes, baking powder, Old Bay seasoning and egg and mix gently.

Shape the crab meat mixture into 8 patties and coat with the cracker crumbs. Fry in a small amount of canola oil in a skillet until golden brown on both sides, turning once. Drain on paper towels.

Yield: *8 crab cakes*

All hotels in Bristol, Kingsport, Johnson City, and Abingdon are booked one year in advance for races. The closest hotel rooms available are in Roanoke, Knoxville, or Asheville.

Marinated Grilled Tuna with Mango Salsa

Tuna

2 tablespoons olive oil
Juice of 2 limes
2 garlic cloves, minced
1/2 teaspoon salt
1/2 teaspoon freshly ground pepper
4 to 6 fresh tuna steaks,
      1 to 1 1/2 inches thick

For the tuna, combine the olive oil, lime juice, garlic, salt and pepper in a bowl and mix well. Pour over the tuna in a sealable plastic bag. Seal tightly and turn to coat. Marinate in the refrigerator for 30 to 45 minutes, turning several times. Let stand until room temperature. Drain, reserving the marinade.

Grill the tuna on a lightly oiled grill rack over high heat for 5 to 7 minutes per side or until the tuna is nearly opaque and springy to the touch, basting occasionally with the reserved marinade. Allow approximately 10 minutes total grilling time per inch of thickness with consideration to personal preferences for rare tuna. Serve with the salsa.

Mango Salsa

1 firm ripe mango, peeled, cut into
      1/4-inch pieces
1/2 cup (1/4-inch) pieces red onion
1/3 cup (1/4-inch) pieces jicama or
      cucumber
2 tablespoons minced fresh cilantro
1 serrano chile, minced, or
      1/2 jalapeño chile, seeded,
      minced
Juice of 1 lime
1/8 to 1/4 teaspoon salt
1/8 to 1/4 teaspoon freshly ground
      black pepper
1/8 to 1/4 teaspoon cayenne pepper

For the salsa, combine the mango, onion, jicama, cilantro, serrano chile, lime juice, salt, black pepper and cayenne pepper in a bowl and mix well.

Yield: *4 to 6 servings*

Tarragon Tartar Sauce

Serve with grilled salmon or tuna.

1 cup mayonnaise
4 anchovies, chopped, or 1 tablespoon
    anchovy paste
1/4 cup tarragon vinegar
1/4 cup fresh tarragon leaves, or 1/4
    teaspoon dried tarragon
3 tablespoons chopped fresh chives
1/4 cup chopped fresh parsley, or
    1/2 teaspoon dried parsley flakes
2 tablespoons Dijon mustard
2 tablespoons rinsed drained capers,
    chopped
1 tablespoon sweet pickle relish
Salt and pepper to taste

Combine the mayonnaise, anchovies, tarragon vinegar, tarragon, chives, parsley, Dijon mustard, capers, pickle relish, salt and pepper in a bowl and mix well. Chill, covered, for 1 hour or longer before serving.

Yield: 1½ cups

Pineapple Mango Salsa

Serve with grilled fish, seafood, or pork.

1 cup 1/4-inch pieces fresh mango
1 cup 1/4-inch pieces fresh pineapple
1/4 cup chopped red onion
1½ tablespoons rice wine vinegar
1 tablespoon chopped fresh cilantro
1 teaspoon minced gingerroot
1/4 teaspoon red pepper flakes,
    crushed

Combine the mango, pineapple, onion, wine vinegar, cilantro, gingerroot and red pepper flakes in a bowl and mix well. Chill, covered, in the refrigerator. May be prepared up to 4 hours in advance.

Yield: 2 cups

Baked Pesto Chicken Bow Ties

16 ounces bow tie pasta
2½ cups shredded cooked
    chicken breasts
1½ cups homemade or commercially
    prepared pesto
1 (10-ounce) can cream of chicken
    soup
1 (4-ounce) jar artichoke hearts,
    drained, rinsed, cut into
    quarters
1 (4-ounce) jar diced pimentos,
    drained
¼ cup drained oil-pack sun-dried
    tomatoes, julienned
1 cup freshly grated Parmesan cheese

Cook the pasta using package directions until al dente; drain. Combine the pasta, chicken, pesto, soup, artichokes, pimentos and sun-dried tomatoes and mix gently.

Spoon the chicken mixture into a 9×13-inch baking dish sprayed with nonstick cooking spray. Sprinkle with the cheese. Bake, covered, at 350 degrees for 35 to 40 minutes or until bubbly. Serve with Caesar salad and French bread.

Yield: *6 to 8 servings*

Larry Carrier and Carl Moore traveled to Charlotte Motor Speedway in 1960 to watch a race, and it was then that they decided to build a speedway in Northeast Tennessee. However, they wanted a smaller model of CMS, something with a more intimate setting, and opted to erect a half-mile facility instead of mirroring the 1.5-mile track in Charlotte.

Fresh Pesto Sauce on Angel Hair Pasta

5 cups fresh basil, large stems
   removed
1½ cups extra-virgin olive oil
½ cup fresh parsley, large stems
   removed
3 or 4 large garlic cloves
3 tablespoons pine nuts (optional)
2 teaspoons kosher salt
1 teaspoon ground pepper
2 cups freshly grated Parmesan
   cheese
12 to 16 ounces angel hair pasta

Combine the basil, olive oil, parsley, garlic, pine nuts, kosher salt and pepper in a blender or food processor container. Process until blended, scraping the side of the container as needed. Add the cheese. Process until smooth. The thickness of the sauce may be adjusted by adding dried basil to absorb any excess oil if desired. Chill, covered, in the refrigerator.

Bring the pesto to room temperature; do not heat. Cook the pasta using package directions; drain. Toss with the pesto in a bowl immediately. Serve with additional Parmesan cheese.

Pesto may be frozen in an airtight container for up to 1 year. Freeze in ice cube trays for individual portions and wrap each portion individually.

Yield: *6 servings*

155

Greek Spaghetti

1/3 cup butter, melted
1/3 cup olive oil
3 garlic cloves, crushed
1/4 cup black olives
8 ounces mushrooms, sliced
8 ounces shrimp, peeled, deveined
8 ounces small scallops
1/3 cup white wine
1/2 teaspoon salt
1/2 teaspoon oregano
1/2 teaspoon basil
1/8 teaspoon cayenne pepper
8 ounces spaghetti, cooked
1/4 cup freshly grated Parmesan
    cheese

Heat the butter and olive oil in a large sauté pan. Add the garlic and olives. Sauté for 3 minutes. Stir in the mushrooms. Sauté for 5 minutes. Add the shrimp, scallops, wine, salt, oregano, basil and cayenne pepper.

Simmer for 15 to 20 minutes or until the seafood is cooked through, stirring frequently. Add the pasta and toss to mix. Spoon into a serving bowl. Sprinkle with the cheese. Serve immediately.

Yield: *4 servings*

Tuscan Pasta Bake

1 red bell pepper
1 yellow bell pepper
8 plum tomatoes, coarsely chopped
1/2 cup fresh basil leaves, chopped
1/3 cup extra-virgin olive oil
2 garlic cloves, finely chopped
1 teaspoon onion salt
16 ounces gnocchi
4 ounces goat cheese, chopped
1/2 cup freshly grated Parmesan
   cheese

Cut the bell peppers horizontally into halves; discard the cores and seeds. Arrange the bell peppers cut side down on a baking sheet. Broil 3 to 4 inches from the heat source until charred. Place in a sealable plastic bag immediately and seal tightly. Let stand for 15 minutes. Peel the bell peppers and coarsely chop. Combine the roasted peppers, tomatoes, basil, olive oil, garlic and onion salt in a bowl and mix well. Let stand at room temperature for 30 minutes.

Cook the gnocchi using package directions until al dente; drain. Combine the gnocchi, roasted pepper mixture and goat cheese in a bowl and toss gently to mix. Spoon into a 9×13-inch baking dish sprayed with nonstick cooking spray. Sprinkle with the Parmesan cheese. Bake at 350 degrees for 20 minutes or until bubbly. Serve with a tossed green salad and crusty bread.

Yield: *8 servings*

157

Work began on what was then called Bristol International Speedway in 1960, and it took approximately one year to finish. Many ideas for the track were scratched on envelopes and brown paper bags by Carrier, Moore, and Pope.

Victory Lap

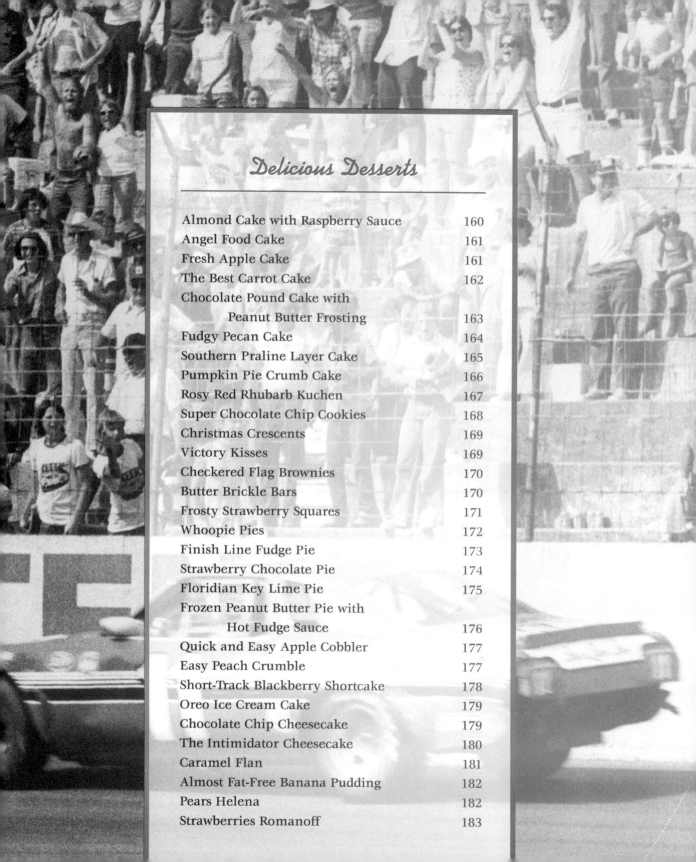

Delicious Desserts

Almond Cake with Raspberry Sauce

This cake was served at the 2000 Drivers' Wives Luncheon.

Cake
1 cup (2 sticks) butter, softened
½ cup shortening
3 cups sugar
5 eggs
2 teaspoons almond extract
1 teaspoon vanilla extract
1 teaspoon salt
1 teaspoon baking powder
3 cups flour
1 cup milk
2 tablespoons amaretto (optional)

For the cake, beat the butter and shortening in a mixing bowl until creamy. Add ½ cup of the sugar and stir. Add 1 of the eggs and stir. Repeat the process with the remaining sugar and remaining eggs. Add the flavorings, salt and baking powder and mix well.

Stir ¾ cup of the flour into the creamed mixture. Add the remaining flour alternately with the milk and mix well.

Spoon the batter into a greased and floured bundt pan. Bake at 325 degrees for 1 hour. Reduce the oven temperature to 300 degrees. Bake for 15 minutes longer. Pour the amaretto over the hot cake. Let stand until cool. Invert onto a cake plate.

Raspberry Sauce
1 pint fresh raspberries, or
*   1 (10-ounce) package thawed*
*   frozen raspberries*
2 tablespoons sugar, or to taste

For the sauce, combine the raspberries and sugar in a food processor or blender container. Process until puréed. Press the purée through a fine sieve into a bowl, discarding the seeds. Serve with the cake. Omit the sugar if using frozen raspberries.

Yield: *12 to 15 servings*

Angel Food Cake

Lynda Petty, wife of Richard Petty

1 cup flour, sifted
1½ cups egg whites (whites of about
    11 or 12 eggs)
1 teaspoon cream of tartar
1½ cups sugar
¼ teaspoon salt
1 teaspoon vanilla extract

Sift the flour 4 more times. Beat the egg whites in a mixing bowl until foamy. Add the cream of tartar and beat until stiff but not dry peaks form. Add the sugar gradually, beating constantly. Beat in the salt and vanilla. Fold the flour into the beaten egg whites. Spoon the batter into an ungreased angel food cake pan. Bake at 325 degrees for 1¼ hours or until the top is brown and dry. Invert on a funnel to cool completely. Loosen the cake from the side of the pan. Invert onto a cake plate. Serve with fresh fruit and whipped cream.

Yield: *12 servings*

Fresh Apple Cake

2½ cups flour
1 teaspoon baking soda
1 teaspoon baking powder
1 teaspoon salt
1 teaspoon cinnamon
2 cups sugar
½ cup vegetable oil
2 eggs
3 cups chopped peeled apples
1 cup (6 ounces) butterscotch chips

Combine the flour, baking soda, baking powder, salt and cinnamon in a bowl and mix well. Combine the sugar, oil and eggs in a bowl and mix well. Add the flour mixture alternately with the apples, mixing well after each addition. Spoon the batter into a greased and floured 11×13-inch cake pan. Sprinkle with the butterscotch chips. Bake at 350 degrees for 50 to 60 minutes or until the cake tests done.

Yield: *12 to 16 servings*

The Best Carrot Cake

Cake
2 cups flour
2 teaspoons baking soda
2 teaspoons cinnamon
1 teaspoon salt
1 teaspoon nutmeg
2 cups sugar
1½ cups vegetable oil
4 eggs
3 cups grated carrots
½ cup chopped nuts

For the cake, sift the flour, baking soda, cinnamon, salt and nutmeg into a bowl and mix well. Combine the sugar, oil and eggs in a bowl and mix well. Add the flour mixture to the sugar mixture and stir until blended. Stir in the carrots and nuts.

Spoon the batter into 2 greased and floured 10-inch cake pans or 3 greased and floured 8-inch cake pans. Bake at 350 degrees for 25 to 30 minutes or until the layers test done. Cool in pans for 10 minutes. Remove to wire racks to cool completely.

Cream Cheese Frosting
3 cups confectioners' sugar
8 ounces cream cheese, softened
Evaporated milk

For the frosting, combine the confectioners' sugar and cream cheese in a mixing bowl. Beat until creamy, scraping the bowl occasionally. Beat in enough evaporated milk 1 tablespoon at a time to achieve a spreading consistency. Spread the frosting between the layers and over the top and side of the cake.

Yield: *10 to 12 servings*

Chocolate Pound Cake with Peanut Butter Frosting

This cake was served at the 2000 Drivers' Wives Luncheon.

Cake
3 cups flour
$1/2$ cup baking cocoa
1 teaspoon baking powder
3 cups sugar
$1^1/2$ cups (3 sticks) butter, softened
5 eggs
1 cup milk
1 teaspoon vanilla extract

For the cake, sift the flour, baking cocoa and baking powder into a bowl and mix well. Beat the sugar and butter in a mixing bowl until creamy. Add the eggs 1 at a time, beating well after each addition. Add the flour mixture and mix well. Stir in the milk and vanilla.

Spoon the batter into a greased bundt pan. Bake at 300 degrees for 80 to 90 minutes or until a wooden pick inserted in the center comes out clean. Cool in pan for 10 minutes. Invert onto a wire rack to cool completely.

Peanut Butter Frosting
3 cups confectioners' sugar
$1/2$ cup creamy peanut butter
$1/4$ cup ($1/2$ stick) butter, softened
3 tablespoons milk

For the frosting, combine the confectioners' sugar, peanut butter, butter and milk in a mixing bowl. Beat until of a spreading consistency, scraping the bowl occasionally and adding additional confectioners' sugar and/or milk for the desired consistency. Spread over the top and side of the cake.

Chocolate Glaze
$1/2$ cup (1 stick) butter
6 tablespoons milk
$1/4$ cup baking cocoa
1 (1-pound) package confectioners' sugar
2 teaspoons vanilla extract

Alternatively, omit the frosting and top the cake with Chocolate Glaze. Heat the butter and milk in a saucepan until the butter melts. Stir in the baking cocoa. Bring to a boil, stirring frequently. Remove from heat. Add the confectioners' sugar and vanilla and mix until of a glaze consistency. Drizzle over the cake.

Yield: *12 servings*

Fudgy Pecan Cake

Cake

1½ cups sugar
¾ cup (1½ sticks) butter, melted
1½ teaspoons vanilla extract
3 egg yolks
½ cup plus 1 tablespoon baking
    cocoa
½ cup flour
3 tablespoons vegetable oil
3 tablespoons water
¾ cup chopped pecans
3 egg whites
⅛ teaspoon cream of tartar
⅛ teaspoon salt

For the cake, line the bottom of a 9-inch springform pan with foil. Brush the foil and side of the pan with butter. Combine the sugar, ¾ cup butter and vanilla in a mixing bowl. Beat until blended. Add the egg yolks 1 at a time, beating well after each addition. Add the baking cocoa, flour, oil and water and beat until blended. Stir in the pecans.

Beat the egg whites, cream of tartar and salt in a mixing bowl until stiff peaks form. Fold the beaten egg whites into the chocolate batter. Spoon the batter into the prepared pan. Bake at 350 degrees for 45 minutes or until the top cracks slightly. The cake will not test done in the center. Cool in pan on a wire rack for 1 hour. Chill, covered, until firm.

Royal Glaze and Assembly

1⅓ cups semisweet chocolate chips
½ cup heavy cream

For the glaze, combine the chocolate chips and cream in a saucepan. Cook over low heat until blended, stirring frequently.

To assemble, remove the side of the pan. Place the cake on a cake plate. Drizzle with the glaze.

Yield: *12 servings*

Southern Praline Layer Cake

Cake
1 cup packed brown sugar
½ cup (1 stick) butter
¼ cup whipping cream
½ cup chopped pecans
1 (2-layer) package devil's food
    cake mix
1¼ cups water
⅓ cup vegetable oil
3 eggs

For the cake, grease and flour two 8- or 9-inch cake pans. Combine the brown sugar, butter and whipping cream in a saucepan. Cook over low heat until blended, stirring occasionally. Pour equal portions of the mixture into the prepared pans. Sprinkle with the pecans.

Combine the cake mix, water, oil and eggs in a mixing bowl. Beat at low speed until moistened. Beat at high speed for 2 minutes longer, scraping the bowl occasionally. Spoon the batter over the prepared layers. Bake at 325 degrees for 35 minutes or until the layers spring back when lightly touched. Cool in pans on a wire rack.

Topping and Assembly
8 ounces whipped topping
1 teaspoon vanilla extract
Chocolate curls

For the topping, combine the whipped topping and vanilla in a bowl and mix well.

To assemble, arrange 1 layer praline side up on a cake plate. Spread with half the topping. Top with the remaining layer praline side up. Spread with the remaining topping. Chill, covered, for 6 hours. Garnish with chocolate curls.

Yield: *12 servings*

Pumpkin Pie Crumb Cake

1 (2-layer) package yellow cake mix
½ cup (1 stick) unsalted butter,
    softened
1 egg
1 (29-ounce) can pumpkin
1 cup sugar
⅔ cup evaporated milk
3 eggs
2 teaspoons cinnamon
½ cup sugar
¼ cup (½ stick) unsalted butter,
    chilled
1 cup chopped pecans

Reserve 1 cup of the cake mix. Combine the remaining cake mix, ½ cup butter and 1 egg in a mixing bowl. Beat at high speed until blended. Press over the bottom of a greased and floured 9×13-inch cake pan.

Combine the pumpkin, 1 cup sugar, evaporated milk, 3 eggs and cinnamon in the same mixing bowl. Beat at medium speed until blended. Spread over the prepared layer. Combine the reserved cake mix, ½ cup sugar and ¼ cup butter in the same mixing bowl. Beat at low speed until crumbly. Sprinkle over the prepared layers. Top with the pecans.

Bake at 300 degrees for 1¼ hours or until set and brown on top. Cool in pan on a wire rack. Cut into squares.

Yield: *20 servings*

Purchase of the land on which BMS now sits, as well as construction of the track, cost approximately $600,000.

Rosy Red Rhubarb Kuchen

Crust
1¼ cups flour
1 tablespoon sugar
1 teaspoon baking powder
½ teaspoon salt
½ cup (1 stick) margarine, softened
2 tablespoons milk
1 egg, beaten

For the crust, combine the flour, sugar, baking powder and salt in a bowl and mix well. Cut in the margarine until crumbly. Add the milk and egg and mix well. Pat the crumb mixture with floured hands over the bottom and ½ to 1 inch up the side of a 9×9-inch baking pan.

Rhubarb Filling
4 cups 1-inch pieces rhubarb
1 (3-ounce) package strawberry
    gelatin

For the filling, arrange the rhubarb over the prepared layer. Sprinkle with the gelatin.

Topping
1 cup sugar
½ cup flour
½ cup (1 stick) margarine, melted

For the topping, combine the sugar and flour in a bowl and mix well. Stir in the margarine. Sprinkle over the prepared layers. Bake at 350 degrees for 40 to 45 minutes. Serve warm with vanilla ice cream. May freeze for future use.

Yield: *9 to 12 servings*

Super Chocolate Chip Cookies

2½ cups flour
1 teaspoon baking soda
½ teaspoon salt
1 cup (2 sticks) unsalted butter,
    softened
¾ cup sugar
¾ cup packed light brown sugar
1 tablespoon vanilla extract
1 tablespoon Frangelico
1 tablespoon coffee liqueur
2 eggs
4 cups (24 ounces) milk chocolate
    chips
1 cup chopped walnuts
½ cup chopped pecans
½ cup chopped macadamia nuts

Combine the flour, baking soda and salt in a bowl and mix well. Combine the butter, sugar, brown sugar, vanilla and liqueurs in a mixing bowl. Beat at high speed until light and fluffy, scraping the bowl occasionally. Add the eggs and beat well. Add the dry ingredients and mix well. Stir in the chocolate chips, walnuts, pecans and macadamia nuts.

Drop the batter by ¼ cupfuls 2 inches apart onto an ungreased cookie sheet. Bake at 325 degrees for 16 minutes or until golden brown. Cool on cookie sheet for 2 minutes. Remove to a wire rack to cool completely.

Yield: *3 dozen cookies*

Christmas Crescents

½ cup (1 stick) butter, softened
¼ cup confectioners' sugar
1 cup sifted flour
½ cup chopped nuts
1 teaspoon vanilla extract
Confectioners' sugar to taste

Combine the butter and ¼ cup confectioners' sugar in a mixing bowl. Beat until creamy. Add the flour gradually, beating well after each addition. Stir in the nuts and vanilla.

Shape the dough by teaspoonfuls into crescents on an ungreased cookie sheet. Bake at 325 degrees for 15 to 18 minutes or until light brown. Cool on cookie sheet for 2 minutes. Remove to a wire rack to cool completely. Sprinkle with confectioners' sugar to taste.

Yield: *1 dozen cookies*

Victory Kisses

3 egg whites
1 cup sugar
1 teaspoon vanilla extract
1 cup chopped pecans
1 cup (6 ounces) chocolate chips
Peppermint extract to taste

Combine the egg whites, sugar and vanilla in a mixing bowl. Beat until stiff peaks form. Fold in the pecans, chocolate chips and peppermint extract.

Drop by tablespoonfuls onto a cookie sheet lined with waxed paper and shape into kisses. Bake at 225 degrees for 25 minutes or until dry.

Yield: *2 dozen kisses*

Checkered Flag Brownies

2 cups flour
1 cup baking cocoa
1 teaspoon baking powder
1 teaspoon salt
1½ cups (3 sticks) butter or
    margarine, melted
3 cups sugar
1 tablespoon vanilla extract
5 eggs
15 small chocolate peppermint
    patties, cut into quarters

Combine the flour, baking cocoa, baking powder and salt in a bowl and mix well. Combine the butter, sugar and vanilla in a bowl and mix well. Add the eggs and mix until blended. Stir in the flour mixture. Reserve 2 cups of the batter.

Spread the remaining batter in a greased 9x13-inch backing pan. Top with the chocolate peppermint patties. Spread with the reserved batter.

Bake at 350 degrees for 55 to 65 minutes or until the brownies begin to pull from the sides of the pan. Cool in pan on a wire rack. Cut into squares.

Yield: *3 dozen brownies*

Butter Brickle Bars

1 (2-layer) package yellow cake mix
½ cup (1 stick) butter, softened
1 egg, beaten
1 (14-ounce) can sweetened
    condensed milk
1 egg, beaten
1 teaspoon vanilla extract
1 cup chopped pecans
1 to 2 cups brickle bits

Combine the cake mix, butter and 1 egg in a bowl and mix by hand until blended. Press over the bottom of a greased and floured 9×13-inch baking pan. Combine the condensed milk, 1 egg and vanilla in a bowl and mix well. Stir in the pecans and brickle bits. Spoon into the prepared pan.

Bake at 350 degrees for 25 to 30 minutes or until the edges pull from the sides of the pan. Cool in pan on a wire rack. Cut into bars.

Yield: *2 dozen bars*

Frosty Strawberry Squares

1 cup sifted flour
$\frac{1}{2}$ cup chopped pecans
$\frac{1}{4}$ cup packed brown sugar
$\frac{1}{2}$ cup (1 stick) butter, melted
2 powdered egg whites, reconstituted
2 cups sliced fresh or frozen
    strawberries
1 cup sugar
2 tablespoons lemon juice
1 cup whipped cream or whipped
    topping

Combine the flour, pecans and brown sugar in a bowl and mix well. Stir in the butter. Spread the crumb mixture evenly in a 9×13-inch baking pan. Bake at 350 degrees for 20 minutes, stirring frequently.

Sprinkle $\frac{2}{3}$ of the crumbs over the bottom of a 9×13-inch dish. Combine the reconstituted egg whites, strawberries, sugar and lemon juice in a mixing bowl. Beat at high speed for 10 minutes or until stiff peaks form.

Fold the whipped cream mixture into the strawberry mixture. Spread in the prepared dish. Sprinkle with the remaining crumb mixture. Freeze, covered, for 6 to 10 hours. Cut into squares.

Yield: *2 dozen squares*

The entire layout for BMS covered 100 acres and provided parking for more than 12,000 cars. The track itself was a perfect half-mile, measuring 60 feet wide on the straightaways and 75 feet wide in the turns, and the turns were banked at 22 degrees.

Whoopie Pies

Cookies
2 cups flour
1 cup sugar
5 tablespoons baking cocoa
1½ teaspoons baking soda
1 cup milk
5 tablespoons shortening
1 egg

For the cookies, combine the flour, sugar, baking cocoa and baking soda in a bowl and mix well. Combine the milk, shortening and egg in a mixing bowl. Beat until smooth. Add the flour mixture and beat until blended. Drop the dough by small tablespoonfuls 2 inches apart onto an ungreased cookie sheet. Bake at 425 degrees for 7 minutes. Cool on cookie sheet for 2 minutes. Remove to a wire rack to cool completely.

Creme Filling
¼ cup shortening
¼ cup (½ stick) butter, softened
½ cup confectioners' sugar
½ cup marshmallow creme
1 teaspoon vanilla extract

For the filling, combine the shortening and butter in a mixing bowl. Beat until creamy. Add the confectioners' sugar, marshmallow creme and vanilla. Beat until of a spreading consistency, scraping the bowl occasionally. Spread over half the cookies. Top with the remaining cookies.

Yield: *20 cookies*

Finish Line Fudge Pie

½ cup (1 stick) butter or margarine
3 ounces unsweetened chocolate
3 tablespoons light corn syrup
1½ cups sugar
1 tablespoon flour
4 eggs, beaten
1½ teaspoons vanilla extract
¼ teaspoon salt
1 unbaked (9-inch) pie shell

Combine the butter and chocolate in a double boiler. Heat over simmering water until blended, stirring occasionally. Remove from heat. Stir in the corn syrup.

Combine the sugar and flour in a bowl and mix well. Stir into the chocolate mixture. Add the eggs, vanilla and salt and mix well. Spoon the chocolate filling into the pie shell.

Bake at 350 degrees for 30 to 40 minutes or until a knife inserted in the center comes out clean. Garnish each serving with whipped cream and fresh strawberries.

Yield: *8 servings*

Strawberry Chocolate Pie

Crust
1¼ cups graham cracker crumbs
3 tablespoons sugar
⅓ cup butter or margarine, melted

For the crust, combine the graham cracker crumbs and sugar in a bowl and mix well. Stir in the butter. Press the crumb mixture over the bottom and up the side of a lightly greased 9-inch pie plate. Bake at 325 degrees for 10 minutes. Let stand until cool.

Chocolate Filling
½ cup semisweet chocolate chips
8 ounces cream cheese, softened
¼ cup packed brown sugar
½ teaspoon vanilla extract
1 cup whipping cream, whipped
1 pint fresh strawberries

For the filling, place ½ cup chocolate chips in the top of a double boiler. Bring the water to a boil; reduce heat to low. Cook until the chocolate melts, stirring frequently. Cool slightly.

Beat the cream cheese in a mixing bowl until light and fluffy. Add the brown sugar and vanilla. Beat until blended. Add the melted chocolate and mix well. Fold in the whipped cream. Spoon the chocolate filling into the baked crust. Chill, covered, for 8 hours.

Reserve 1 whole strawberry. Cut the remaining strawberries into thick slices. Place the whole strawberry in the center of the pie and arrange the strawberry slices in a decorative pattern around the whole strawberry.

Topping
2 tablespoons semisweet chocolate chips
1 teaspoon shortening

For the topping, combine 2 tablespoons chocolate chips and shortening in a saucepan. Cook over low heat until melted, stirring frequently. Drizzle over the top. Chill until serving time.

Yield: *8 servings*

Floridian Key Lime Pie

Crust

1¾ cups graham cracker crumbs
2 tablespoons sugar
6 tablespoons butter, melted

For the crust, combine the graham cracker crumbs and sugar in a bowl and mix well. Stir in the butter. Pat the crumb mixture over the bottom and 1 inch up the side of a 9-inch springform pan. Chill for 1 hour.

Key Lime Filling

3 egg yolks
1 (14-ounce) can sweetened condensed milk
½ cup fresh Key lime juice or Persian lime juice
1 tablespoon lemon juice
2 teaspoons grated Key lime zest or Persian lime zest
3 egg whites
2 tablespoons sugar

For the filling, whisk the egg yolks in a bowl until blended. Add the condensed milk, lime juice, lemon juice and lime zest and whisk until mixed. Beat the egg whites in a mixing bowl until foamy. Add the sugar gradually, beating constantly until soft peaks form. Fold the beaten egg whites into the lime mixture. Spoon into the prepared pan. Bake at 325 degrees for 15 to 20 minutes or until set and light brown. Cool in pan on a wire rack. Chill, covered, for 8 hours.

Topping

1 cup whipping cream
1 tablespoon confectioners' sugar
½ teaspoon vanilla extract
Lime slices, cut into quarters

For the topping, beat the whipping cream in a mixing bowl until slightly thickened. Add the confectioners' sugar and vanilla and beat until soft peaks form. Remove the side of the pan. Dollop the whipped cream around the edge of the pie. Garnish with lime slice quarters.

Yield: *8 servings*

Frozen Peanut Butter Pie with Hot Fudge Sauce

Chocolate Crust
3/4 cup crushed chocolate wafers
1/4 cup sugar
1/4 cup (1/2 stick) unsalted butter, melted

For the crust, combine the wafer crumbs and sugar in a bowl and mix well. Stir in the butter. Press the crumb mixture over the bottom and up the side of a 9-inch pie plate. Chill in the refrigerator.

Peanut Butter Filling
8 ounces cream cheese, softened
1 cup crunchy peanut butter
3/4 cup sugar
1 tablespoon vanilla extract
1 1/2 cups chilled whipping cream

For the filling, combine the cream cheese, peanut butter, sugar and vanilla in a mixing bowl. Beat until smooth. Beat the whipping cream in a mixing bowl until stiff peaks form. Fold the whipped cream 1/4 at a time into the peanut butter mixture. Spoon the filling into the prepared pie plate, mounding in the center. Freeze for 2 hours or until firm. May be prepared up to this point 1 day in advance and stored, covered, in the freezer.

Hot Fudge Sauce
1/2 cup sugar
1/2 cup whipping cream
1/4 cup (1/2 stick) unsalted butter
2 ounces unsweetened chocolate
1/2 teaspoon vanilla extract

For the sauce, combine the sugar and whipping cream in a saucepan and mix well. Bring to a boil; reduce heat. Simmer for 6 minutes; do not stir. Remove from heat. Add the butter and chocolate and stir until blended. Stir in the vanilla. Spread over the top of the pie. Garnish with miniature peanut butter cups.

Yield: *8 servings*

Quick and Easy Apple Cobbler

Nancy Wood, wife of Len Wood

6 tablespoons butter
3 cups ¾-inch chunks peeled apples
½ to ¾ teaspoon cinnamon
1 cup flour
1 cup sugar
⅔ cup milk

Spray a 9×9-inch baking dish with nonstick cooking spray. Heat the butter in the prepared dish in a 350-degree oven until melted. Toss the apples with the cinnamon in a bowl. Arrange the apple mixture in the prepared pan.

Combine the flour and sugar in a bowl and mix well. Stir in the milk. Spoon the batter over the apples. Bake at 350 degrees for 45 to 55 minutes or until light golden brown. Serve warm topped with ice cream or whipped cream.

Yield: *6 to 9 servings*

Easy Peach Crumble

A favorite recipe from Carol Frank, Buffy Waltrip's mother. Buffy is the wife of Michael Waltrip.

3 cups sliced peeled South Carolina
    peaches
2 tablespoons Fruit-Fresh
1 tablespoon cornstarch
1 cup self-rising flour
1 cup sugar
2 teaspoons cinnamon
½ cup (1 stick) margarine

Toss the peaches with a mixture of the Fruit-Fresh and cornstarch in a bowl. Spoon the peach mixture into a greased 2-quart baking dish.

Combine the self-rising flour, sugar and cinnamon in a bowl and mix well. Cut in the margarine until crumbly. Sprinkle the crumb mixture over the peaches. Bake at 350 degrees for 1 hour.

Yield: *6 servings*

Short-Track Blackberry Shortcake

This is especially fun to prepare after a day of picking blackberries.

2 cups flour
4 teaspoons baking powder
1½ tablespoons sugar
1 teaspoon salt
5 tablespoons butter, cut into pieces
⅔ cup milk
2 tablespoons butter, melted
6 cups fresh blackberries
1 cup sugar
¼ teaspoon salt

Combine the flour, baking powder, 1½ tablespoons sugar and 1 teaspoon salt in a bowl and mix well. Cut in 5 tablespoons butter until crumbly. Add the milk gradually, stirring until the dough adheres. Knead the dough on a lightly floured surface for 1 minute. Roll into a ½-inch-thick 7×14-inch rectangle. Brush with 2 tablespoons melted butter.

Combine the blackberries, 1 cup sugar and ¼ teaspoon salt in a bowl and toss gently to mix. Spoon half the berry mixture over the rectangle. Roll starting from the short end to enclose the filling. Arrange the roll seam side down in a 7×11-inch baking dish sprayed with nonstick cooking spray. Spoon the remaining blackberry mixture around the roll.

Bake at 375 degrees for 40 to 50 minutes or until a wooden pick inserted in the center comes out clean. Slice and serve warm with vanilla ice cream.

You may substitute blueberries for 3 cups of the blackberries if desired.

Yield: *6 to 8 servings*

Oreo Ice Cream Cake

1 (20-ounce) package Oreo cookies,
    crushed
2 cups confectioners' sugar
1 cup (2 sticks) butter
4 eggs, beaten
1/2 gallon vanilla ice cream, softened
Whipped cream

Reserve 1 cup of the cookie crumbs. Spread the remaining cookie crumbs in a 9×13-inch dish. Combine the confectioners' sugar, butter and eggs in a saucepan. Cook over medium heat until thickened, stirring frequently. Spoon over the prepared layer. Spread with the ice cream. Sprinkle with the reserved cookie crumbs. Freeze, covered, until serving time. Top each serving with whipped cream.

Yield: *15 servings*

Chocolate Chip Cheesecake

1 1/2 cups finely crushed chocolate
    sandwich cookies (about
    18 cookies)
1/4 cup (1/2 stick) butter or margarine,
    melted
24 ounces cream cheese, softened
1 (14-ounce) can sweetened
    condensed milk
3 eggs
2 teaspoons vanilla extract
1 cup (6-ounces) miniature chocolate
    chips
1 teaspoon flour

Combine the cookie crumbs and butter in a bowl and mix well. Pat the crumb mixture over the bottom of a 9-inch springform pan. Beat the cream cheese in a mixing bowl until light and fluffy. Add the condensed milk. Beat until smooth. Add the eggs and vanilla and beat until blended.

Toss 1/2 cup of the chocolate chips and flour in a bowl. Stir the chocolate chip mixture into the cream cheese mixture. Spoon into the prepared pan. Sprinkle with the remaining 1/2 cup chocolate chips. Bake at 300 degrees for 1 hour or until the cheesecake springs back when lightly touched. Cool in pan on a wire rack. Chill, covered, until serving time. Remove the side of the pan and place the cheesecake on a cake plate. Garnish as desired.

Yield: *10 to 12 servings*

179

The Intimidator Cheesecake

Serving this elegant cheesecake at a dinner party is guaranteed to send the hostess on a trip to victory lane.

Crust

1¼ cups chocolate wafer crumbs
¼ cup (½ stick) plus 1 tablespoon butter, melted
2 tablespoons slivered almonds

For the crust, combine the wafer crumbs and butter in a bowl and mix well. Press the crumb mixture over the bottom and 1 inch up the side of a 9-inch springform pan. Sprinkle with the almonds. Chill in the refrigerator.

Filling

8 ounces semisweet chocolate
24 ounces cream cheese, softened
1 cup sugar
3 eggs
1½ tablespoons instant coffee granules
2 tablespoons Kahlúa
1 teaspoon vanilla extract
1½ cups sour cream

For the filling, place the chocolate in the top of a double boiler over cold water. Bring the water to a boil; reduce heat. Cook over low heat until the chocolate melts, stirring frequently. Beat the cream cheese in a mixing bowl until light and fluffy. Add the sugar gradually, beating constantly until blended. Add the eggs and beat until smooth. Beat in the chocolate. Crush the coffee granules with the back of a spoon until of a powdery consistency. Combine the coffee powder, Kahlúa and vanilla in a bowl and mix well. Add to the cream cheese mixture. Beat until blended. Fold in the sour cream. Spoon the cream cheese mixture into the prepared pan. Bake at 350 degrees for 1 hour. Turn off the oven. Let the cheesecake stand in the oven with the door partially open for 30 minutes. Remove to a wire rack to cool. Chill, covered, for 8 hours.

Topping

½ cup whipping cream
1 tablespoon confectioners' sugar
Chocolate curls

For the topping, beat the whipping cream in a mixing bowl until soft peaks form. Add the confectioners' sugar gradually and mix well. Remove the side of the pan and place the cheesecake on a cake plate. Top each serving with whipped cream and chocolate curls.

Yield: 10 to 12 servings

180

Caramel Flan

1 cup sugar
8 eggs
2 (12-ounce) cans evaporated milk
2 tablespoons vanilla extract
¼ teaspoon salt
Orange slices

Pour enough water into a 9×13-inch baking pan to measure 1 inch. Place the baking pan on the middle oven rack in a 350-degree oven.

Heat ½ cup of the sugar in a heavy skillet until the sugar begins to melt. Cook until the sugar turns amber in color, stirring constantly. Pour the hot caramel mixture into a 6-inch ring mold or loaf pan, tilting the pan to coat the bottom evenly.

Beat the eggs in a mixing bowl until frothy. Add the remaining ½ cup sugar, evaporated milk, vanilla and salt. Beat until blended. Pour the custard into the prepared ring mold.

Set the ring mold or loaf pan in the preheated baking pan. Bake for 50 minutes. Remove the mold to a wire rack to cool. Chill in the refrigerator.

Run a sharp knife around the edge of the flan. Place a plate upside down over the top of the mold and invert quickly. Garnish with orange slices.

Yield: *8 servings*

Almost Fat-Free Banana Pudding

Arlene Martin, wife of Mark Martin

This recipe was created by Mark's mother, Jackie, and is one of his favorite desserts.

3 cups skim milk
2 large packages fat-free sugar-free
    vanilla instant pudding mix
1 cup fat-free sweetened condensed
    milk
16 ounces fat-free whipped topping
1 package reduced-fat vanilla wafers
2 or 3 large bananas, sliced

Combine the skim milk, pudding mix, condensed milk and whipped topping in a mixing bowl. Beat until smooth. Alternate layers of the vanilla wafers, bananas and pudding mixture in a large trifle bowl until all of the ingredients are used, ending with the pudding mixture.

Yield: *6 to 8 servings*

Pears Helena

1/3 cup heavy cream
1/4 cup superfine sugar
4 ounces German's sweet chocolate,
    chopped
1 ounce unsweetened chocolate,
    chopped
Vanilla ice cream
6 canned pear halves

Combine 2 tablespoons of the cream and the sugar in a double boiler. Cook over hot water until the sugar dissolves, stirring frequently. Remove the double boiler from the heat, leaving the top of the double boiler over the hot water. Add the chocolate and stir until blended. Beat in the remaining cream until smooth. Cover to keep warm.

Spoon the desired amount of ice cream into each of 6 dessert bowls. Arrange 1 pear half over each serving of ice cream. Drizzle with the warm chocolate sauce.

Yield: *6 servings*

Strawberries Romanoff

A beautiful and easy finale for a summer dinner party.

3/4 cup Grand Marnier or Triple Sec
Juice of 2 lemons
2 teaspoons sugar
3 cups fresh strawberry halves
3/4 cup sour cream
1/4 cup honey
1 teaspoon cinnamon
2 cups whipping cream
2 tablespoons confectioners' sugar
4 whole strawberries

Combine the Grand Marnier, lemon juice and sugar in a bowl and mix well. Add the strawberry halves and toss to coat. Combine the sour cream, honey and cinnamon in a bowl and mix well.

Spoon equal amounts of the strawberries into parfait glasses. Pour 1/4 of the sour cream mixture over each serving.

Beat the whipping cream in a mixing bowl until soft peaks form. Add the confectioners' sugar and mix well. Top each serving with whipped cream and 1 whole strawberry. Serve immediately.

Yield: *4 servings*

Fred Lorenzen won the pole for the first race at BMS with a speed of 79.225 mph.

Active League Members

Lisa Adkins
Deborah Adler
Bambi Akard
Laura Bassett
Amy Booher
Stacey Bright
Angela Broglio
Tracey Brown
Bambi Bruce
Bonnie Burke
Elizabeth Burriss
Rebecca Burton
Mandy Butterworth
Andrea Carroll
Whitney Caudill
Katie Chesser
Tracey Chitwood
Amy Christian
Lynn Couch
Fran Crumley
Molly Deckard
Brandi Detrick
Mona Durban

Shawna Feeley
Cindy Ferguson
Lori Fletcher
Lynn Fuller
Brenna Gillispie
Melissa Harrison
Genia Helms
Karen Hyatt
Yolanda Istfan
Kathy Keen
Susan Key-Higinbothom
Desiree Kiethan
Danielle Kiser
Kim Leonard
Leigh Littleford
Amber McMurray
Rita Mercier
Debra Miller
Katie Morrell
Sabrina Morton
Alicia Mumpower
Kristi Nab
Julie Rainero

Rainey Rainero
Jill Rogers
Lee Ann Ruth
Suzanne Senter
Amy Shuttle
Katy Sikorski
Whitney Singleton
Corey Smith
Kenan Stead
Lisa Stevens
Melissa Steward
Katie Sword
Joy Thacker
Melinda Upchurch
Emilie Varney-Stafford
Cindy Vetter
Holly Vining
Carter Manning Wade
Angie Williams
Kristen Wood
Valerie Zochowski

Other Contributors

Doris Adair
Katharine Bergmann
Jennifer Borsch
Becca Cooper
Jane Copenhaver
Mandi Dennis
Nancy Estes
Rita Estes
Laurie Everett
Katy Ford

Deborah Gessner
Marjorie Hallenbeck
Donna Hudgens
Sharilyn Jones
Sharon Jones
Terra Kistner
Carrie Layfield
Corina Oakley
Gay Robinson
Frances Rowell

Deborah Stallard
Cathy Stivers
Bill Thomas
Catherine Traynham
Danea Walters
Cathy Wingate
Vonda Wingate
Kimberly Wishon-Powell
Marjorie Wolfenden
Susan Zickler

2005-2006 Sustainers

Cina Adams
Landy Adams
Nancy Arnold
Virginia Arnold
Robin Bagnall
Patricia Bane
Virginia Barker
Ann Barton
Carol Biegler
Thelma Blair
Zanna
  Blankenbeckler
Alice Blanton
Sally Blanton
Joday Blevins
Tracie Blevins
Dixie Bowen
Katharine Bowie
Linda Brittle
Penny Bruce
Marjorie Buchanan
Mary Ellen Buhls
Connie Bullock
Martha Jean
  Bundy
Teresa Burkholder
Sara Burleson
Rose Marie Burriss
Arnell Byers
Vivian Calcote
Susan Caldwell
Eddythe Carr
Nancy Clark
Annette Cochran
Dorothy Cooper
Peggy Cooper
Joan Crockett
Luann Crockett
Kaye Crutchfield
Jane Culp
Dena Cunningham
Mary Curtin
Jane Daniel
Rebecca

Davenport
Nancy DeFriece
Jan Detrick
Merle Dickert
Vicie Dotson
Beverly Dunn
Susan Early
Terry Eckley
Laura Eskridge
Carol Everhart
Eileen Everitt
Dee Flannagan
Dorothy Fleming
Rebecca Fletcher
Wilma Fletcher
Carolyn
  Fletcher-Helton
Angie Frye-Shaffer
Jackie Fuller
Rita Gayewski
Ann Gillenwater
Marica Gilliam
Jane Godsey
Shirley Godsey
Anne Goodpasture
Ann Greear
Reba June Green
Janice Greene
Mary Groseclose
Deborah Gwaltney
Doris Hagey
Doris Harkrader
Lucy Harkrader
Tracey Harmon
Jill Harrison
Jo Ann Hatcher
Fan Hepburn
Mary Margaret
  Herzog
Gay Hillman
Nancy Hoffer
Angela Hopkins
Amy Hopper
Eloise Horner

Beth Hovious
Emily Hubbard
Rhonda Hurt
Lettie Jackson
Wendy Jacobs
Ilene Janson
Amelia Jarrard
Missy Johnson
Chris Jones
Ida Jones
Mary Jones
Margaret Kearfott
Diana Kegley
Molly Keller
Pam Kerr
Carolyn King
Jeanne King
Julie King
Margaret King
Ronan King
Ruth King
Betty Kuhnert
Barbara Sue
  Kurre
Jean Lacy
Isabelle Ladd
Sandra Larkin
Joyce Lawson
Patricia Lawson
Beth Layton
Debra Leonard
Jean Lewis
Evelyn
  Lindamood
Joan Link
Bonnie Liskey
Mary Ann Little
Kathleen Littleford
Nancy Marney
Meredith Massie
Pam McFarlane
Dian McIlwain
Ann McInturff
Stefanie McKenzie

Debbie McMillin
Jennifer
  McQueary
Karen McSharry
Mary Jane Miller
Lynn Monahan
Bettye Moneyhun
Robin Moneyhun
Chrissy Mullins
Dianna Mullins
Peggy Mullins
Julie Murthy
Anne Neese
Peggy Nicar
Barbara Oakley
Joyce Oakley
Judy Olson
Kathleen Overbay
Pam Ownby
Jewel Parker
Nancy Jane Parks
Pereda Paty
Aleeta Pearson
Karen Pennington
Sharon Penny
Barbara Pippin
Lea Powers
Bettye Purcell
Mary Beth Rainero
Mary "Butch"
  Rainero
Betty Rae Reuning
Pat Rhea
Linda Riley
Brennan Rockett
Dottie Ross
Jeanne Rowley
Martha Jean Sams
Cindy Samuel
Carol Sandoe
Helen Scott
Clarice Senter
Dana Sherwood
Peggy Shields

Emma Shipley
Carla Shumate
Helen Shupe
Donna Sikorski
Carolyn Slagle
Judy Slaughter
Barbara Smith
Gwen Smith
Deborah Snyder
Karen Spear
Dianna Stone
Mary Stuart
Lori Sweat
Susan Tanner
Diane Thomas
Julie Thomas
Linda Thompson
Lisa Tickle
Winona Tipton
Frances Trammell
Sandra Vaughn
Linda Waldron
Nancy Wallace
Chris Walling
Susan Walling
Alice Ward
Vicki Ward
Musser Warren
Eileen Weberling
Billie Whisnant
Margaret Whitaker
Betsy White
Dawn White
Lisa White
Kristina Willis
Peggy Winston
Nancy Wood
Ann Woods
Laura Young
Audrey Zaidi

Index

Start Your Ovens

Cooking the Way It Ought'a Be
From the Junior League of Bristol

P.O. Box 1599

Bristol, Virginia 24203-1599

Please send _____ copies of *Start Your Ovens* at $19.95 each $ ————————————————

Add 5.0% sales tax at $1.00 each $ ————————————————

Postage and handling at $4.00 each $ ————————————————

Total $ ————————————————

Name _____

Street Address _____

City _____ State _____ Zip _____

Method of Payment: [   ] Visa   [   ] Check payable to the Junior League of Bristol

Account Number _____ Expiration Date _____

Signature _____

Photocopies will be accepted.